259
TI50

VENTURES IN YOUTH WORK

HENRY N. TANI

Ventures
in
Youth Work

THE CHRISTIAN EDUCATION PRESS
1505 Race Street   Philadelphia 2, Pennsylvania

Library of Congress Catalog Card Number: 57-9060

PRINTED IN THE U.S.A.

EDEN PUBLISHING HOUSE

DEDICATED

TO MY MOTHER

WHOSE PRAYERS HAVE SUSTAINED ME

TO ROSE, MY WIFE

WHOSE DEVOTION HAS ENCOURAGED ME

AND TO RICHARD, STEVEN, JOHN, AND CHRISTINE

FOR WHOM I CHERISH THE EXPERIENCES DESCRIBED

IN THIS BOOK

Table of Contents

Foreword

TWO QUESTIONS that youth workers in the church often ask are, "How do we get young people to come?" and "How do we hold their interest?" To get and to hold the elusive teenagers becomes the challenge and the task of ministers, teachers, and advisers. Similarly, there is a constant plea for adult persons who will give time and effort to serve the church in teaching and counseling young people. Our lay members hesitate to give this kind of service to the church, yet most certainly we feel the pressure for more and better adult workers with young people.

Because the population bulge of children is now pouring into the junior high department and the youth fellowship program, the local church will do well to gird itself for an aggressive, and we hope an adequate, ministry to the teenagers. This book may give some indication of the answers to the two questions quoted above, but I am convinced that there is no easy answer. Only by prayer and perseverance can youth and adults together work out each problem at the local level.

Into the preparation for writing this book have gone several years of stimulating contacts and experiences in both the denominational and interdenominational world. My work in the office of the Board of National Missions of the Evangelical and Reformed Church in the immediate postwar years has given me increased appreciation for aggressive churchmanship. To the persons with whom I was then associated, I am very grateful. More recently I have been enjoying the fellowship of dedicated men and women on the Committee on Youth Work of the

National Council of Churches. This committee, with the many relationships which grow out of it, has indeed been my "school on youth work." I am greatly indebted to the many persons with whom I labored to plan and present the best in Protestant youth work. This includes, too, the young people of the several denominations who come together in the United Christian Youth Movement's General Council. My association with the youth leaders of the Congregational Christian Churches in planning for church school curriculum has also contributed to my grasp of our Christian education task.

To the young people and their adult workers in my Evangelical and Reformed Church who have patiently suffered under my prodding, I must confess that I have probably learned more from them than I gave. In this connection, for their helpful counsel I express my gratitude to my immediate associates, Miss Ethel A. Shellenberger, Rev. Edward L. Schlingman, and Herman C. Ahrens, Jr. To Dr. Franklin I. Sheeder who encouraged me to write this book, and to Dr. Fred D. Wentzel who edited it, I give my thanks. To my secretary, Mrs. Clara Utermohlen, who has faithfully managed the work entrusted to my office, I am deeply indebted. There are certainly others who contributed to this book, including those who have so kindly read the manuscript and made helpful comments. Finally, to my wife and children who carry on at home under the rigorous demands of my work, I express gratitude for their constant understanding.

This book, then, is a product of these years of concern, hope, prayer, and work with youth. We face the tremendous task of confronting our teenagers with the Christian gospel, of setting the stage so that each person may make a decision of commitment to God through Jesus Christ. It is an urgent venture, both for the teenagers and for us.

HENRY N. TANI

Philadelphia
February 1957

CHAPTER ONE

The Unique Task of the Church

THE CAST: Mr. Jackson, pastor of St. John's Church
Fred Morrow, active youth member at St. John's
James and Betty Howard, young couple, parents of two
children, only recently active in church
THE SETTING: The pastor and Fred Morrow are visiting the
Howards.

Pastor: Jim, it's been good to have you join St. John's Church.

Jim: Why, thank you. Betty and I discussed the matter of
church membership and since we now live in Betty's neighborhood, St. John's seemed to be the logical choice.

Betty: I had not been too active in church since I graduated
from high school. Somehow I had a feeling that I wasn't of
much use to the church.

Pastor: Well, Betty, even if you didn't appear too active,
St. John's always felt it had a claim on you. After all, you've
attended Sunday school here for many years.

Betty: And I've enjoyed the fun our young people's group
had. The hayrides, the skating parties, Christmas carols—I
thrill all over as I relive those moments.

Jim: In my church experience I remember little else besides
the parties and refreshments. Oh yes—those business meetings
when we discussed by the hour whether we should have hot
chocolate or pink lemonade.

Fred: Do you mean to say that even in those days you had long business meetings?

Jim: Let's not make it seem so long ago, Fred. But, yes, while I seem to forget what I learned in Sunday school and in the youth meetings, I do remember the long business sessions.

Betty: Now that I think of it, I believe it was being with the church gang that I liked most.

Fred: What do you mean by the church gang? Our kids now come from scattered places, and we see each other only when we come to church.

Pastor: This is one of those things that modern transportation and shifting population are doing to us, Fred. Not so long ago, our people were more closely settled, and the church was the center of most social and community activities.

Fred: Mr. Jackson, don't you think we should tell Mr. and Mrs. Howard why we came?

Jim: Yes, Mr. Jackson, you've got us guessing.

Pastor: Why, of course. As you know, for some time I have been serving as adult adviser to the youth fellowship for the regular Sunday night meetings.

Fred: And he's been very helpful, too. But we feel that we shouldn't use up his time the way we young people do.

Pastor: I have been feeling the pressure of other duties that I have as pastor of the church.

Fred: So the youth group has been thinking about getting new adult advisers to help relieve Mr. Jackson.

Pastor: To make a long story short, Jim, we have come to ask you and Betty to serve as adult advisers for the young people of our church.

Betty: Who, us?

Jim: You're not kidding, are you, Mr. Jackson?

Fred: Honest, Mr. Howard, our youth fellowship talked it over, and we've decided we want you and Mrs. Howard to be our adult advisers.

Betty: This is fantastic! We don't know the first thing about working with young people.

Jim: And besides, it's not exactly clear to me just what the church's job is in working with young people.

Betty: I had never dreamed that we should be adult advisers to young people. I can't even imagine the responsibilities that go with the job.

Jim: Aside from helping with the scout troop, I hardly know the young people of the church.

Betty: Of course, I did some substitute teaching of the junior high class, but I felt so inadequate as a teacher.

Jim: What seems most embarrassing to me is that I don't know too much about this business of being a Christian myself, though I am perfectly willing to learn.

Betty: And we have little children. Where do we find the time?

Pastor: Whoa! whoa! Not so fast. You are right in raising these questions, so let's look at them. Now Betty, you were asking about working with young people.

Fred: Our senior high kids figure that we've just got to have adult advisers. Without an adult person around, we find ourselves doing the same old thing. Mostly we need adults to restrain us from going too wild, to give us new ideas, and yet be willing for us to try our own way at our own speed.

Betty: That sounds reasonable. I remember the one thing about the adult adviser we had when I was a teenager was her understanding ways.

Jim: But teenagers are hard to understand. Don't they become aloof and mysterious in their adjustment to adolescent growth?

Pastor: I pray for and worry about our young people, but I fear that as a minister I have become removed from them. In my presence they are ladies and gentlemen—they put on a very good show. Yet I am sure I do not get really close to them personally.

Fred: That's a funny thing to say. While we respect you, Mr. Jackson, I guess it's true that we don't talk to you about personal matters. It's only about church things we talk in your presence.

Betty: To change the subject, I've noticed, now that I'm older, how much alike young people want to be. This shows in their clothes, their activities, their vocabulary, and even in their thinking. There must be tremendous pressure to want to belong to the crowd.

Fred: Yeah—who wants to be a square?

Pastor: It has been my deepest concern that we treat these young people, not as children, and again not as adults. We must provide enough guidance, and yet let them make their own decisions and carry out their own plans.

Fred: Somehow your sermons don't seem to say anything to me, Mr. Jackson. I try awfully hard to understand, but you don't connect with me.

Jim: On the other hand, the same sermons mean so much to me. I catch on, and I must say, Mr. Jackson, you've said some powerful things to me.

Pastor: Why, thank you, Jim. There's something about church that makes us depend upon traditional ways. For instance, have you noticed how so many teachers lecture to their Sunday school pupils? We seem to depend upon telling, telling, and more telling.

Betty: I know many people who come to church to be entertained. You know—good music, good food, good fun, good films, good sermon.

Fred: Yeah, man. We come to church to have a ball.

Pastor: What did you say?

Jim: Are you implying, Mr. Jackson, that the traditional ways don't work? What do you suggest?

Pastor: Young people, for instance, must make some very definite decisions about jobs. How is the high school student guided in his choice of his life vocation? For that matter, what is he intending to do with his life?

Betty: But that doesn't seem to be any concern of the church. After I finished school, I found a job, then I found a husband. Having a family of my own now, I think I've arrived.

Jim: But Betty, there must be something more. There ought to be a sense of destiny, a feeling of purpose, yes, even some definite plan for life.

Fred: Boy, I could use some help.

Pastor: Well, now, I don't propose that our own church become an employment bureau, but I do say that unless St. John's instills in each person a sense of Christian vocation in whatever job he chooses, I will have failed as a minister, and St. John's will have failed as a church of Jesus Christ.

Jim: That would be a departure from the traditional. What else do you have in mind?

Pastor: Every young person must choose a lifemate. Oh yes, and some persons will choose not to marry. But for most persons, the question of "Whom will I marry?" means a major life decision.

Betty: Where is this a concern of the church? For me, it was a high moment to be married by you in our church. Beyond that, I had no feeling that St. John's cared.

Jim: Could it be that this is why the church encourages social activities for young people? Here, the fellows can meet the girls in a wholesome atmosphere.

Fred: Mr. Jackson, that meeting when you showed the film-strip "How About a Date?" was really helpful. But what's the Christian angle to all this boy-girl stuff?

Pastor: Frankly, I feel we have a great responsibility in presenting the Christian attitude toward sex. The dignity of persons, the respect for self, the care of our bodies, the relation between man and woman, the sacredness of the marriage vow, the sanctity of the home, the strength of wholesome family life —all this and more are of religious, yes, of Christian importance.

Fred: How will all that you say mean anything to me as a teenager?

Betty: For one thing, Fred, it appears to me that high school students today are too much bent on going steady, and at such an early age!

Fred: You mean, I've got to give up my steady girl friend? Gosh, everybody has a steady. Is there anything wrong in that?

Jim: No, Fred, it's not going steady that we are concerned with. Perhaps we are more anxious to help you grow socially, to meet lots of people, and to have a wide circle of acquaintances before you narrow your friendship to one person.

Fred: Come to think of it, one of the best discussion meetings we had was the one on Protestant-Catholic romance. Getting married sure can be a religious headache.

Pastor: You are getting the drift of my concern. Many people find their marriage partner, get married, establish a home, and rear a family without ever considering the need of putting God into every step.

Betty: Perhaps what we lack is a clear understanding of our Christian beliefs. I feel as if I sailed through Sunday school and confirmation class right into church membership without anything important happening to me.

Jim: This is what I mean about my embarrassment about being a Christian. Some place in my teen years I think I stopped growing—that is, spiritually speaking.

Pastor: Our church prides itself on stressing an educated membership, and to that end, we have a fairly thorough series of classes for the early teenagers.

Fred: I joined the church when I was 14, but I'm still not sure whether I can give an intelligent answer about what I believe.

Pastor: Fred, here is one reason why I struggle within myself about teenagers and the way in which we receive them into adult membership. While their intellectual, physical, and social growth continue through their high school years, we give no aggressive program to stimulate their spiritual growth.

Jim: I don't know just what you have in mind, but I can see that "What do I believe?" is another of the major questions we've got to help young people answer.

Betty: This conversation is all well and good, but what does the church have, really, to make it so strategic in working with young people?

Pastor: You've put your finger on a sensitive spot, Betty. I would say that the first unique feature is the compulsion on the Protestant church to communicate the gospel of Jesus Christ to all persons.

Jim: Is this what you meant in your recent sermon about the urgency of having God's way acknowledged by mankind? In fact, isn't this the theme of many of your sermons?

Fred: For us young people, then, the church wants us to hear and understand the gospel.

Betty: Why do you use the word "compulsion," Mr. Jackson? St. John's Church doesn't seem under pressure to make me face up to the life and teachings of Jesus Christ.

Pastor: It's remarks like yours, Betty, that make me shiver and quake at the immensity of our task, and the inadequacy of my preaching. Yet I have utmost faith that God touches the life and destiny of each person.

Jim: As a member of the church, perhaps I should become more conscious of God, and learn to understand his role. I believe you used such words as creator, sustainer, redeemer, and judge.

Fred: If the church could lead me to face up to the Christian gospel, I'd be scared stiff. But I'm willing. Bring it on.

Pastor: The second unique feature of the Protestant church is that we have a rich history, from way back in Old Testament days, through Christ, the disciples and the early church, through the Reformation, and the personalities of our own denomination.

Fred: Is this what you call the heritage of our church?

Pastor: And there is more. Here in our community, St. John's has had years of consistent leadership, a favorable reputation, good facilities, and an established membership who have given, and still give time, talent, and money.

Betty: Are you describing our St. John's Church?

Jim: I'm new here, myself, but I've had a sneaking suspicion that this church didn't sprout over night.

Pastor: Consider the church building. It is situated on a busy corner of town, with a spire that can be seen for miles. Betty, your forefathers three or four generations ago gave a generous portion of their funds to make this building possible.

Betty: And I've heard Grandfather talk about the struggle they had to pay the minister's salary and to keep the building in good condition.

Jim: I suppose the faithful members year after year gave money to do missionary work around the world, as well as to help the needy in our own country.

Fred: And even now, I feel especially proud when I see the responsible people in our community come to worship regularly at our church. This says something to me.

Pastor: It is for these reasons that we are blessed with a favored position in the community—a responsible membership, a building dedicated to serve the community, and a spirit of sacrifice and service to all persons. For our part, St. John's must give the best it can to the community. Our work with young people must therefore be of high caliber.

Betty: I am particularly happy to have had those family life institutes recently, Mr. Jackson. Having two pre-school youngsters, we are anxious to build the kind of family life that will make us good parents.

Pastor: The family life institute is one of several responsibilities of the committee on Christian education at St. John's. What started out with only the Sunday church school program now covers a wide range of activities including weekday religious education, vacation church school, summer camps and conferences, hobby and athletic clubs, related agencies like the scouts, fellowship groups for young and old, and of course, the youth program.

Fred: You mean the youth fellowship program belongs to the Christian education committee?

Pastor: Really, all activities for the young people make up the youth fellowship program of the church. This includes the Sunday morning church school, regular church services, evening youth fellowship group, as well as all other groups and activities involving young people.

Jim: Your explanation seems to rule out a separate league or society of young people who are organized, and hold meetings for themselves.

Betty: Then the third unique feature of the Protestant church is this Christian education program.

Pastor: The fourth is that the church is a redemptive fellowship. When Jesus called together his disciples, he fired them with a sense of divine purpose, and challenged them to love, work, and worship together. This little band of ordinary men revolutionized the world. We have inherited this special kind of fellowship.

Jim: What has this to say about St. John's?

Fred: At summer youth conference we talk a lot about the Christian community. Somehow we felt a responsibility for each other that I've never known before.

Betty: Going to church with our children is a chore by itself for me. I don't have time or occasion to worry and work with other members.

Pastor: But it is precisely this kind of casual and impersonal relationships we have in our church that must be changed. We need to recapture the spirit of intensive fellowship among our members.

Jim: While I don't understand all you've said, Mr. Jackson, what are we supposed to do with the young people at St. John's? Are there some purposes which indicate what ought to be going on?

Fred: Our youth fellowship has a statement of purpose in official language. But briefly, there are three points. We want to understand God's will and develop spiritual depth for truly committed life.

Betty: That sounds like Christian faith and belief.

Fred: Second, we want to engage in meaningful activities, and to show Christianity to the community and the world.

Jim: Hmmm. Missionary study, service projects, and community action.

Fred: Third, we want to relate ourselves to other Christians.

Pastor: Food, fun, and fellowship. That was a quick and brief resume of the purpose of the youth fellowship. But for me, I see one over-all purpose in the church's ministry to young people—that is to provide the setting so that God can touch and change lives, and bend them to his will.

Jim: That sounds simple and straightforward enough—provide the setting—touch and change lives—bend to his will. Good enough.

Pastor: Now Jim and Betty, what do you think of taking over the adult advisers' job?

Betty: Of course, Jim and I haven't talked this over, but the pressure of time seems to make it difficult to say yes.

Jim: For my part, I am tempted to consider it for a short while—one year isn't too long.

Pastor: Now, Jim, I don't want to make this sound like a short and easy job. I was thinking in long terms, perhaps a five-year assignment for the two of you.

Betty: Five years! That's almost a life-time!

Jim: Do you realize what you're asking? That would cut right into our personal schedules. Our obligations now are so heavy—take my Thursday night bowling, for instance.

Betty: And Tuesday is our bridge club. And we visit Jim's folks out in the country every month.

Jim: I'm looking forward to Sundays with our children. And we visit Betty's folk every other week.

Betty: Women's circle meetings come once a month, and Jim's men's club at church is every third Wednesday, too. Oh no, I don't see how we can give the time.

Jim: And besides, we don't have the training. Surely there must be others in the church who could do this much better than we.

Fred: Gosh, we thought surely you would give this a try. While you may not know too much about the youth fellowship program, we hoped you'd be willing to learn.

Pastor: The young people chose you because of your friendly personalities. As a young couple, you have been an example and even perhaps idols for them.

Jim: But five years!

Pastor: We talked tonight about traditional ways. Really, I should ask for your whole life for service to God and to mankind. I am asking for only a chunk of it now.

Betty: But no one has ever asked this much of us before. Tell me again, how much time will this take?

Fred: Well, we'd like you at every meeting, Sunday nights.

Jim: That could mean some week nights for preparation, I guess.

Pastor: And you could anticipate personal conferences for advice and consultation.

Jim: How about cooperation from parents?

Fred: This is rough. Many parents just want us out of the way.

Betty: We don't have to be concerned with the Sunday morning church school classes, do we?

Pastor: Yes, you do, Betty. You won't have to teach in the morning, but you should coordinate the evening activities with the morning lessons, or at least know what is going on. And this means that you should attend the monthly meetings of the church school workers.

Jim: I can see my bowling nights going out the window.

Pastor: Don't think we're asking you to do this alone. The committee on Christian education to which you will be responsible, has assured an adequate budget, and the church council will provide necessary facilities to support your work.

Fred: And the kids in youth fellowship have agreed to provide baby-sitting service for you, free, any time.

Jim: Five years!

Pastor: Oh, we'll settle for three, if necessary. I don't want you to get the idea that you can throw this job off lightly. Perhaps the greatest satisfaction I can promise you is to watch these young people grow into mature Christian adulthood. And because you are doing God's work, he will give you strength and guidance.

Betty: Let us think this over, please. We'll give you our answer on Sunday.

Fred: I do hope you'll take it. I promise you the cooperation of the young people.

Pastor: And may God be with you as you consider this challenge. We'll look for your answer Sunday.

CHAPTER TWO

What Makes Teenagers Tick?

ADOLESCENTS PASS THROUGH a trying stage between the ages of 12 to 20, when they change from children to adults. What are some of the things we can expect of teenagers, and what are the pressures on their lives?

(1) *This is a period of tremendous growth.* The obvious changes are in the physical maturation of the boys and girls in their early teen years. Almost overnight these early adolescents add inches and pounds, and perplex their parents with healthy appetites and demands for more adequate clothing.

Though growth is a continuous process for all individuals, each person grows at his own rate, which may be slower or later than the average, and yet will be quite normal for him. As a rule, girls mature one to two years earlier than boys, and this causes any number of embarrassing situations for the junior high group.

Growth is not even, but often comes in spurts and leaps. The internal changes and growth may not be as evident. The total growth to balanced physical maturity takes most of the teen years.

Certainly heredity has much to say about the growth pattern of the child. Family customs and eating habits, traditional observances and relationships all affect the maturation of the individual.

In the years of rapid growth, the adolescents show much

activity and prolonged excitement. While they may have their awkward moments, they are the graceful athlete and dancer, and exert much physical energy in self-determined projects. It is therefore not surprising that these same persons show such inactivity and laziness when family chores are suggested. Growth calls for moments of quiet, rest, and long hours of sleep.

There is also intellectual growth in the adolescent years. With each additional year, the teenager can cope with more difficult and intricate problems and affairs, and in fact he may surpass the knowledge of his parents. He becomes anxious and willing to discuss and argue his views, and becomes quite adept in presenting a case or a question. Longer periods of concentration, more personal research, and greater originality mark the growing adolescent.

(2) *The adolescents live in their own teenage world.* Because they are highly conscious that they are no longer children, and are in turn rebuffed by the adults, our teenage population lives in a world of its own. This teenage society is marked by a high degree of similarity in the vogue of the day, whether it is a slang expression, certain styles of clothing, or some mysterious ritual known only to themselves. There is much talking in their circles, and an air of busyness.

The wish to conform allows the teenager to enter the sacred society. To belong, to be accepted, to be recognized—these are his secret desires. The fact that everyone is doing it determines what demands he makes on his parents for increased freedom, later hours, more money, and greater privileges.

When a problem arises, the teenager turns to his peers, the members of his age-group, and talks out the situation. Great reliance is placed upon the findings of his age-mates, and this in fact is a healthy process. Of course, the decisions of his peers may not always find acceptance by the adults.

Not everything, however, is pleasant within this teenage

world. Invariably a select few become a closed circle and make it difficult for others to attain a position within the circle. The clique can be made of those who live in certain social or economic areas, or of athletes or student council officers. The "in-group" may maneuver itself into a controlling position in the teenage world. Clubs and social organizations also attempt to foster a sense of belonging to specific groups. Certainly, age and grade make considerable difference, and one can readily note the strata of such groupings.

Usually, the older teenager would much rather belong to a group of his own age or grade, and scornfully looks down on those younger than he. On the other hand, the younger teenager would like nothing more than to be socially acceptable with those who are two to three years older. This sensitive relationship indicates to church leaders the unity which can be had within certain age groups, and also the advisability of separating the junior highs from the senior highs. Rather than struggle with junior high activities and conversations which are below their level, senior highs usually slip out of the fellowship group and from other youth activities.

Probably a major force operating within the teenage world is the romance that blooms, and the hand-holding that abounds. The pleasure that boys and girls have in each other's company, the delight in choosing and being chosen, and the exhilaration of the first date open a new vista in life. This is an important stage in growth. Secret crushes and big moments come and go, but an ever-present concern is to know that one can rate with a girl, or is acceptable to a boy. Through all these trying days, the teenager must learn the social graces of making conversation, of courtesy, of consideration and friendliness.

Inevitably, some persons here and there are left out of this teenage world. This tragedy in their lives may not be reflected in their words or deeds, but in their inner hearts they cry in anguish for acceptance.

(3) *The adolescents declare independence.* They struggle to cut the apron-strings that bind them to their parents. The well-adjusted person is one whose independence from home and parents comes about naturally, gradually, and happily. But the change is not easy.

Understandably, all parents are concerned for the welfare and safety of their children. Parents somehow cannot accept the idea that their children are becoming adults. Only reluctantly do fathers and mothers yield at this point or that, and even so, the process may be painful.

What are the most common areas of conflict between teen-agers and their parents? Disagreements are usually on these subjects: going out on school nights, late hours, school grades, use of family car, choice of friends, spending money, and jobs at home. From the teenagers' point of view, these are crucial matters, representing their status as dependable persons or irresponsible children. They are confused by inconsistent remarks, which vary from "Please act your age" to "You are too young to be wearing that."

While they do want as much freedom as they dare to ask, teenagers are frankly lost and bewildered when they are given complete freedom. The teenager needs specific limits within which he can operate. Such limits represent parental interest in his welfare and it is most assuring to know that father and mother do care. Sometimes, of course, he interprets the limits as group pressure, and then he is inclined to rebel against them. One revealing conclusion of a study of adolescent boys 14 to 16 years of age is that these boys rely heavily on parental authority, indicating that they do not yet trust their inner controls.

Another sign of independence in adolescents is to test what adult authorities have been telling them. Thus, for instance, the religious teachings of the church become subject to sharp criticism. With what qualms did we listen to a girl express her doubts about the Apostles' Creed! And yet she was revealing her inability to take everything for granted, and had to be satisfied by her own searching. Parents and teachers find that simple statements are refuted, and must be proved. In fact, teenagers may deliberately do the opposite of what is expected, to demonstrate how independent they are.

When the charge of irresponsible behavior is lifted, it comes as a breath of fresh air to find the teenager who shows remarkable self-control in a tight situation, a considerateness not often seen in adults, thoughtfulness and tenderness toward the elderly and the shut-in. Independence comes in leaps and bounds, but it comes!

(4) *Adolescents face conflicting standards.* In his struggle to become adult, the teenager looks to the world about him to find the guideposts of adult-like behavior. Thus the world of entertainment, magazines and newspapers, the actions and attitudes of adults around him, and the pressure of prevailing thought and custom set the standards. These influences are now developing a generation of young people who take drinking as part of gracious living, cheating as a normal mark of competitive life, and fast driving as the usual method of traveling.

Our culture glorifies mechanical gadgets, the accumulation of things, and the power of military might. The fact that our service personnel abroad misbehaved sexually reflects the fact that our culture tolerates such behavior stateside; drunken brawls and black market techniques were taught to eager eyes and ears in the comfortable homes of our land. Such elements of the secular world seem to the teenager to deny the gospel of Christ, but he also sees truth, decency, mercy, and love exhibited in the life about him.

Parents, teachers, adult workers, and ministers influence the spiritual quality, the emotional tone, the inter-personal responsibilities, and the inner goodness of persons. Faith in mankind, the respect for property, and the mutual dependence of people and races persist as eternal landmarks for each generation.

(5) *The adolescents have anxious moments.* We suspect that there is considerable time spent by our teenager in moody introspection. Granted that he is much in need of love, understanding, and acceptance, that he wishes to belong, to be recognized, and to count for something, he nevertheless has agonizing moments of doubt. If any or all of his secret desires are not achieved, he will quickly try to adjust by securing attention and acceptance by methods which may be quite annoying.

In his efforts to throw off childhood ways, he may face any number of frustrating experiences in the adult world. He cannot secure a job because of inexperience or age or size; he cannot drive a car because he is not granted a license until he has reached legal age; he cannot marry because he is not economically free.

The adolescent may worry a great deal about war and its consequences. He realizes that he may be called for military training, and this may be puzzling and fearsome. Whether he will be successful in work, in marriage, in social life, and in becoming an adult may prove to be awesome. The subject of death and dying is gripping. The teenage girl wonders most whether she will be married happily, and if so, then she wonders about her capacity for the tasks of motherhood. Whether the current school grades are good or not may bring one crisis after another. Making and losing friends, the ability and inability to get dates, having or not having a pleasant home life, all add to perplexing moments of youth.

(6) *The adolescents want adult-like experiences.* More than anything else, the teenager craves an adult-like responsibility. Thus, to hold a job, even a minor one, is to be needed. He will take a reasonable assignment that is within his grasp and understanding. It may be for this reason that the teenagers enter into committee work, conduct meetings, or carry out projects.

Trying to be like an adult has affected the socializing and

romance of our teenagers. In as brief a period as the ten years since the second world war, it is estimated that our young people have begun their love-making experiences one and two years earlier than their elder brothers and sisters did. This acceleration of entering into adult-like experiences comes with the greater mobility of people, of longer trips, of greater stimulation brought by way of television and movies.

Through the mass media of the movies, television, and radio, our teenagers imagine themselves in the adult culture. The disc jockey "speaks to them" and has considerable influence over adolescent minds and emotions. Phonograph records and sheet music surround our young people with an aura of worldly sophistication.

AGE GROUPINGS

For a more effective program, the young people in our churches are usually divided into three age-groupings. These are the junior highs, ages 12-13-14, grades 7, 8, and 9; the senior highs, ages 15-16-17, grades 10, 11, and 12; and the post-high or older youth, those beyond high school, ages 18 to 24.

A growing trend is to divide the six years of junior high-senior high into two-year groupings. This would place the 7th-8th graders in junior high, the 9th-10th graders in middle high, and 11th-12th graders in senior high. Such a division takes account of the relatively advanced status of the 9th grader, and provides some similarity in program and activities for the two older groups, middle high and senior high, although it keeps them separate.

The local public school situation will help determine whether your church should observe the 3-3 break (grades 7-8-9 junior high, and 10-11-12 senior high), the 2-4 division or the 2-2-2 arrangement.

JUNIOR HIGH

Let us note some of the characteristics which distinguish the junior high from the middle and senior high.

(1) *Physical.* These are the years when rapid growth from childhood to adolescence takes place. Because some persons grow faster and taller than others, the range in development in this group is most extreme. As we have indicated, girls generally mature physically two years earlier than boys, and this makes them appear larger. This brings the girls an earlier social awareness, and an apparent intellectual advantage.

Junior highs have a tremendous store of energy which makes them restless and mischievous. They are apt to be rough in their play, to be reckless with furniture, to break rules without conscience, and to be heartless in teasing. They go for heavy eating, and will come to any function for the refreshments.

Because of the uneven and rapid growth of individuals, both boys and girls will be very sensitive about their relative size and development. The tall girls as much as the short boys will appear uncomfortable, while the girls who develop more slowly wonder why they do not show the womanly features that their friends have.

(2) *Social.* Junior highs have a very strong desire to belong, to be accepted. The gang tendency is powerful. To be in step with their age-mates in matters of clothes, tastes, interests, and abilities is paramount. They are cruel to those who do not conform.

In their desire to be noticed, and yet not to be too forward, the girls go in for long giggling spasms. Boys for their part pick on each other, use worship programs to make airplanes, and throw a girl's shoes out of her reach. Both boys and girls would like very much to be accepted by the senior high young people, and look upon them with hero-worship eyes.

The girls are quite ready and willing to hold hands, go steady, and dance. The boys, by and large, are quite reluctant to be paired off. The common sight is to find them hiding behind the piano. Yet these same junior highs are very active in scout work, in athletics, in school and club life, with music lessons, hobbies, and other interests.

While many junior highs are still closely related to family activities, they are beginning to exert their independence. For instance, they choose not to participate in family visiting, and would rather stay home. They become secretive about their coming and going, and become arrogant and rude to their parents.

Similarly, they appear to have no respect for other adult persons. Church school teachers of this age-group find that discipline is a major concern. On the other hand, the same junior highs show great dependence upon adults for information and guidance.

(3) *Intellectual.* Junior high persons have a very short span of concentration, and can therefore not sit long at a meeting or in worship. Their intellectual background is not great enough, nor sufficiently integrated into their own experience to enable them to share in worthwhile and helpful discussion.

They do well in drama, music, crafts, project work, small-committee activities, choral speech, and similar group functions. Junior highs do not need the stimulation of large gatherings, nor of distant places.

(4) *Spiritual.* While junior highs may be in preparation for church membership, their concepts and ideas are vague and uncertain. They may have a grasp of biblical facts and some church history, but their sense of Christian commitment is in an early stage. It is also at this time that many parents permit young people the freedom of choice, of staying or separating from the church. Many do leave.

SENIOR HIGH

Now let us consider the traits which identify the senior high young people.

(1) *General Maturity.* In the senior high years, the young people have achieved a balance of maturity. Their physical growth has come to full blossom; their skill and grace become evident in their athletic activities. Their social adjustment has become more stabilized; both boys and girls are capable of interesting and satisfying social times. Intellectual grasp becomes more positive; senior highs can now participate in meaningful and profound discussions. They can sit through a one-hour lecture, and be socially responsible at meetings and functions away from home.

(2) *Independent Judgment.* Senior highs have been encouraged to do their own thinking, and to come to their own decisions. They have thus come some distance from parental control. Instead of repudiating parents, they are now willing to talk things over, man-to-man. In matters of religious and spiritual teachings, the senior highs ask pertinent questions and desire to find their own answers. They enjoy independent inquiry, and respond to social concerns and missionary responsibility.

In their relation to adult leadership, senior highs prefer to make their own decisions, and to learn by their errors. They request that adult leaders be handy with information and suggestions, and recognize that they need to be spurred on by adults on occasion.

(3) *The Future Beyond High School.* With adulthood in sight, senior high young people face the problems of marriage and jobs, of college and military service. They are frankly fearful. They wonder how they will adjust to new situations. They are also achieving some sense of financial independence,

with many of them holding part-time or regular jobs. Going steady has given some of them the security of social acceptance. Senior highs respond best to adult-like situations and challenges.

OLDER YOUTH

What then are the marks of those who are out of high school?

(1) *Independent of Parents.* Older youth are relatively free of parental control. Though they may still live in their parents' home, older youth come and go to their social, work, and school functions without reporting details to their parents. They are no longer children. They assume an adult role in their homes.

(2) *Same Age, but Different Interests.* While the ages 18 to 24 include the older youth category, older youth are involved in many different classifications. These include the employed and the unemployed, the military and the civilian, newly-married and single, with or without children, those away from home and those living at home, the college students living at home and those away from home. The senior high crowd that was so well-knit before high school graduation is now dispersed geographically, and in the various ways just indicated.

(3) *Problems of Adjustment.* Older youth do share similar concerns. These include friendship and marriage, education and vocation, recreation and moral decisions, faith and churchmanship, adult responsibility and citizenship. They are quite unsettled. While they enjoy their freedom, they are looking for their niche in community life.

TASKS OF AN ADOLESCENT

In recent years, psychologists and other specialists have made considerable strides in the study of growing persons. A pre-school child, for instance, must achieve such abilities as talking, dressing himself, feeding himself, associating with children outside of the home. Some of these tasks are imposed upon him.

While there are normal growth and physical development, there are also social expectations and demands for each stage in life. Such expectations of our cultural society are called "developmental tasks." The authors Jenkins, Bauer, and Schacter, in their book *Teen-Agers* have identified seven such tasks for the adolescent person. Each teenager must achieve the tasks with some degree of facility before he can move on to satisfactory adulthood. Lacking the accomplishment of any of these tasks is considered a handicap, for then an adult person will still be wrestling with an adolescent situation. Briefly stated these are the tasks:

(1) To acquire a set of values
(2) To learn social skills
(3) To accept oneself as a boy or a girl
(4) To understand and accept one's body and bodily changes
(5) To learn to get along with family members
(6) To decide upon and prepare for a life work
(7) To learn to become a responsible citizen

The obvious reaction is to turn the burden of this job to the public schools. Through the educational processes, a trained teacher with all the resources at his command can provide the guidance and counsel which each person needs. The individual teenager himself undoubtedly makes some effort to achieve some of these tasks, with or without guidance, from good or poor associations.

Of this we can be certain, that some of these tasks need adult guidance and motivation. Your church has a storehouse of theological and cultural background, plus some other desirable advantages, which can add dimension and scope to each of these tasks. Within the church, there are adult persons who strive to improve persons and situations; there is a group of like-minded young people whose activities are wholesome; there is a compulsion of direction and purpose. All of these factors working together can be of tremendous influence for each teenager.

In light of these seven tasks, and the description of the adolescent we noted above, an unshakable duty is placed upon every adult leader. A Christian interpretation of each task, a Christian motivation in its accomplishment, and a sense of personal dignity and social responsibility in coping with it—these are the plus elements which you and your church can provide. This is a Christian education function in your church.

CHAPTER THREE

Opportunities for Growth

WHAT DIFFERENCE does it make whether a group of people sit in a circle or in straight rows? Must the teacher do all the preparation for a Sunday morning's lesson? What does it signify when young people tend to sit in the back rows at their own fellowship meetings? What are some clues to more effective teaching in our church situations?

INVOLVE THEM

The magic key to secure cooperation, better attendance, and high interest is to involve every single individual in all the processes imaginable. To be involved means that one is in the activity at hand, and wonder of all wonders, he is then learning. He not only learns painlessly, but enjoys the learning process. But there is more in the involved-learning situation: he makes changes for the better, for the higher. Let us see.

(1) *Involve them in setting goals and aims.* When the church school class receives a new study book for the months ahead, it would be strategic and highly desirable for the teacher and the class to scan the material together, and make some notations. Certain long-range planning like the renting of a film, securing a resource speaker, or doing research can be discussed at this early stage. If the teacher does all this himself, the members of the class may properly shrug their collective shoulders and claim lack of concern and responsibility. They had no part in the planning.

Likewise in the evening fellowship program, how much more meaningful its activities and meetings will be if the total group has a share in its over-all plans. A chance remark about supporting the missionary budget of the church can very well become the springboard for a major discussion. The snowballing effect may result in some venturesome goals: to do three one-act plays, the proceeds to be their extra offering, and to make a conscientious study of their own church's missionary outreach. When such a decision is truly their own, the young people will more honestly support all phases of this project.

(2) *Involve them in working out details.* Once the goals and aims are set, the details must be agreed upon. Small committees can do a more efficient job and come out with better solutions than a whole group deciding whether to serve this or that for refreshments. If the question at hand is how to present the topic of church membership, the planning committee will need to think in terms of a special guest speaker, parent participation, audio-visual resources, or a panel of their own members. This is a healthy process because the young people can see their own decision unfolding into specific plans.

Again, the side-products of these sessions are the give-and-take of personalities and ideas, the appreciation of intimate camaraderie, and the gaining of new insight and knowledge.

(3) *Involve them in actually carrying out assignments.* It should fall on each person to do his share of the total task, or work in rotation, as the case may be. If the church school class agreed that two members in turn were to carry the basic load of discussion, then when one's turn came, he could not easily duck out of his responsibility. Knowing that others are also involved, he is more apt to do his part. If he were pounced upon without warning and asked to do a job of this sort, he could very well be sick that Sunday morning.

When a major project like an Easter sunrise service and

breakfast is planned and each person is assigned to a committee, chances for 100 per cent participation are increased.

(4) *Involve them in the program itself.* Every effort should be made so that each person has some significant part in the big event. It may be mimeographing the program, making posters, playing the piano, singing in the choir, preparing the refreshments, handling money, caring for furniture, projecting the film, conducting the discussion—these may suggest the many possible assignments for the occasion.

(5) *Involve them in the evaluation and review.* The cycle of events is not over until the group has had a chance to review in a leisurely way the processes, the difficulties, the successes and the impact of the series of lessons, or the play, or whatever project the group completed. It is entirely possible that in the revelation of certain facts, and the findings of certain members, the evaluation session may be of the most value.

Let us outline what this procedure of involvement can mean in the case of a youth group planning a new year's eve watch-night service.

Step 1: At the planning sessions early in September, the young people agreed that the Watch-Night service should be a major evening in the holiday season. Pressure for the affair came from those who wanted to celebrate this holiday in a festive, and yet meditative mood. That there would be many college students and service personnel home for the holidays suggested increased participation. Some even indicated that they might have holiday guests who would join in the fun.

Step 2: Anticipation already ran high as the appointment of these committees was completed: general coordination, publicity and invitation, facilities and clean-up, recreation, worship, food and refreshments, decoration, special music, and so on. A series of two or three meetings of committee chairmen were called to double-check progress and coordinate the activities. This tentative schedule was determined:

9:00-10:00   Informal games, board games, ice-breakers
10:00-11:00 Active games, relays, square dances, folk games
11:00-11:45 Refreshments, song session
11:45-12:30 Watch-night worship; special music
12:30- 1:00 Clean-up; good night

Step 3: Each committee then proceeded to do its part, making preparations and contacts. The membership roll was scanned again to make certain that every possible person, both active and inactive, was assigned to one of these committees.

Step 4: On the big night each person knew he had a hand in the decisions and the preparations. He had a significant job tonight—whether it was bringing the record player, or reading Scripture. This was his night, his program, his group, his church. He couldn't help but be there, with bells on.

Step 5: Within one week after the event the committee chairmen met to report, to review, and to evaluate. All finances were accounted for, the borrowed equipment was returned, and outside participants were thanked. The high and low points of the evening were discussed, and notations were made of new talents uncovered, friendships made, and prospective members found.

LEVELS OF LEARNING

There is a definite one-two-three sequence in helping young people learn. Some may think of this as a pyramid-type structure. The lowest level represents the use of words in talking. The second level is the use of pictures and the seeing. The third level involves physical and mental activity in acting out and creating situations, while the highest level is in actual participation in first-hand experience with the subject matter. The higher the level, the better the learning.

To picture this in another way, one may think of a person surrounded by several layers of protection. To talk to him is to penetrate the outside layer; to show him a picture, the next; to have him act or feel, the next; and finally *he* is reached when he is personally and actively engaged. Learning is best achieved when the young person is so immersed in the subject, so upset by the frustrations, so enthused in his search, that he uses all his powers of communication—words, sight, mind, and feeling.

(1) *Listening is basic.* Fundamental in all teaching situations is the use of words. The teacher talks to give instructions, to tell a story, to present a point of view. The sermon, the lecture, the speech, and even the church school lesson depend upon one person talking to an audience.

For young people, the use of words to communicate an idea is inadequate since some words are too difficult, and some ideas are beyond their range. Within a teenage group, there is a wide spread of maturity, and a straight talk may or may not convey the substance of the message.

The biggest obstacle in the use of the lecture method is that the audience takes a spectator attitude, and forces the speaker to entertain and perform. There is little sense of cooperative search for the truth. The polite audience may appear attentive, but their minds may be far afield. Nevertheless, the lowest or basic level requires the use of words.

(2) *Watching and seeing increase understanding.* The use of audio-visual tools brings the world into our circle of young people. With films, filmstrips and records, we see the beauty of the world, the concern of the church, or the life of biblical days. Through stories and legends, biographies and history, we relive the struggle and successes of people through the ages.

There is a tremendous impact of television, radio, the movies and the theater on our daily lives. To get both the seeing and the hearing senses to concentrate on the story or the message increases the grasp of understanding. Advertisers insist on repetition to attract and hold attention to their products.

Church groups also have the advantage of seeing dramatic portrayals of religious events and situations which carry the Christian message. On occasion, colorful and majestic pageants are presented. The fortunate congregation which invites a missionary "sees" the effort required in bringing the Christian witness to various mission fields. Through all of these channels, your young people are confronted with the task of the church, the implications for your congregation, and the challenge to young people.

The emotional impact is certain to bring a desirable response, with increased gifts to missionary causes, concerted effort in collecting and sending relief goods, and a new awareness of the church efforts at home and abroad. In these exposures, young people identify themselves with persons and situations. Through vicarious experience of this sort, a new sympathy and understanding are achieved. To see is to understand more clearly.

The weaknesses in stopping at this watching-and-seeing level are several. Despite the entertainment and instruction which are derived from audio-visuals, drama, and personalities, the members of the audience may still remain passive spectators. The emotional response achieved may be temporary. The most desirable learning changes attitudes, changes lives, changes the mood and tenor of the group.

(3) *Acting and doing are learning tools.* The third level of learning requires your young people to move away from the comfortable spectator role to the more adventurous active situations. This calls for initiative and imagination, for creative opportunities and time-demanding sacrifice. Yes, there is also trial and error, and the need for making personal adjustments with other persons.

Consider a dramatic presentation. The Easter play requires selection of a cast, many rehearsals, adaptations to local facilities and personalities, conference to determine lights and properties, and a continuous effort to make the production honest and real. Through this effort, the learning process is moving at high gear.

To illustrate a story or incident, one can assign to a group of young people the task of pantomiming, using puppets, creating a skit, doing a radio or television broadcast. In the spirit of fun and experimentation, new insights will be found.

When your young people "publish a newssheet" as of a given time in history or situation, they will do research, use their imagination, their talents, and achieve a new sense of mastery of the subject. Games, food, and festivals from other cultures imported and adapted to the local scene contribute to mission study and a new appreciation.

These illustrations suggest the better type of learning situation.

(4) *Active participation is the best learning.* Ultimately the best teaching method is to project the person into the midst of the problem or subject matter. Direct experience cannot be had from film and speeches. First-hand contact and visits, personal research and interviews, on-the-spot discussions and face-to-face exposures to life situations are by far the most desirable learning opportunities.

When a teenager is responsible for the presentation of a class lesson or topic discussion, for recreation or for worship, for a work project or service activity, he is on the highest learning level. This suggests that the major burden of preparation and presentation of lessons and topics should be borne by one or several of the young people.

This also suggests that some subjects which teenagers do not normally choose must be introduced and considered. Here is the place where the adult person should make his contribution by suggesting that certain topics which young people may have overlooked are worth trying. Indeed an honest study of possibilities should involve all young people, and not only the leader of the day.

The church and adult workers must provide the setting and opportunities for these learning experiences. Here are some observations:

• Insist on youth participation in the life of the congregation—the decision-making on the annual budget, membership on committees and councils, assuming a fair share of membership responsibilities, singing in the choir, mimeographing the weekly bulletin, an occasional house-cleaning or landscaping project.

• As much as possible, spread the responsibility of preparing for and conducting church school and youth meeting functions to the young people. Make certain that instructions are clear, that adequate guidance is provided, and that high standards are expected.

• Consider group visits and exposures to institutions, offices, persons, events, and locations which come naturally into the realm and interest of our young people. Such a venture should be undertaken on the basis of an expressed desire of the young people. Be sure to follow a trip of this kind with a full-dress discussion and evaluation.

• Take advantage of issues which are close to teenage life. These are the pressing questions of boy-girl relations, parent-youth tension, school life situations, jobs and college, frictions arising from racial integration, and so on. Be alert to actual incidents, and provide time and opportunity for leisurely and careful consideration of all implications. The Christian sense of forgiveness and reconciliation must pervade all conversations. Full participation in discussion and research is to be encouraged.

• Some honest work activity which brings young people into face-to-face contact with people and situations is within your reach. A weekend work-camp in the community, a summer caravan experience, youth-to-youth visitation evangelism, house-to-house religious preference surveys, visits to shut-ins and the aged, and the like will sharpen the role of the church.

• A concentrated inquiry into the fundamentals of Christian faith and beliefs is in order. Hence a series of Bible studies—not lectures, a review and evaluation of a good book, the full implications of stewardship and Christian vocation, some soul-searching into the demands of Christian commitment, are potent areas for intensive study.

THE SUNDAY SCHOOL ANSWER

Other observations are pertinent here. Church people tolerate a conversational atmosphere of artificial goodness, of superficial cordiality, and a dishonest integrity. Take, for instance, the young people's discussion on race relations. After much prodding, they may quote Scripture to indicate that all men are created of God, that Paul wrote about the Jews and the Gentiles, that Jesus befriended the Samaritan woman at the well. The young people will recall the time the Negro minister spoke, on a race relations Sunday, and the isolated instance when a Negro family worshiped in their church. This kind of polite talk can go on and on, and usually on any subject.

We choose to call this the "Sunday school answer." The discussion is proper and easy. The minister is pleased, the teacher is satisfied, and the teenagers have disposed of another meaningless subject.

Not so. Race relations is a burning issue in our day, and whether it affects certain areas in our nation or our attitude to people around the world, your church youth must face the hard realities of the gospel and its compelling message to its bearers. This calls for honest search into our confusion and fears, doubts and hesitations, hopes and aspirations. We must insist on digging deep, to square our thoughts with our beliefs, to acknowledge shortcoming and weaknesses.

Be alert during the discussion in church school class or youth meeting. See how cleverly your young people avoid the issues, cloud the situation, and defend their position. In all fairness to our young people, let us be thorough in our presentations and expect a sound and adequate discussion on every subject.

This requires an atmosphere conducive to honest and open conversation. The best situation is provided by a small group of eight to ten persons, who have become fairly well acquainted with each other over a period of time. The group should have various experiences together, playing and studying beyond the scheduled hours on a Sunday morning or the evening meeting.

The sense of belonging once established and the fear of ridicule removed, the members of such a small group can soon go beyond the usual surface conversation, reach into personal convictions, and begin to think and act as members of the redemptive society. The loving, forgiving spirit, the desire to share concerns and seek Christian solutions are the fruits of good adult guidance. The real learning comes in the enlarged vision, deepened understanding, the changed view, and yes, the converted soul.

A good discussion, the clash of personalities, the varying points of view, the yielding and agreeing on certain issues, the welding and fusing of common thought, the creation of the "sense of the meeting"—these are the ingredients of honest teaching and learning.

ROLE-PLAYING

Of the many devices and techniques of securing wide participation and a new look at problems, we suggest the use of role-playing and the buzz-group.

Role-playing creates a make-believe situation to present a real problem to the group. This is particularly effective in considering inter-personal relations—parent-youth, boy-girl, race

relations, and so on; and in rehearsing—asking for a job, inviting newcomers to church, and so on.

Take for instance the vexing problem of mixed marriage.
The young Protestant girl wants parental consent to marry a
Catholic friend. The parents are divided on the subject, and on
this basis the setting is established. When the situation is clearly
grasped, volunteers are asked to take the roles of the four characters. Have them come forward and sit around a table. Give
each one of them the name of the person whose role he is
taking. Permit them a moment to review their situation and
setting, and to see their roles clearly.

Assign one of them to be the central person around whom
the conversation turns. In this instance, the girl is the logical
person, and she has the burden of proving her point. It would
be well to have not more than four characters, and clearly defined opposite views. Insist that each person "forget himself"
and use words and expressions normal to the role he plays.

The listening group is requested to be particularly observant.
For instance, one half may concentrate on arguments in favor
of giving consent, the other half on those opposed. When this
preliminary preparation is done (and it need not take more than
five minutes), then the attention is focused on the role-players,
and the discussion leader fades out of the picture.

This unrehearsed spontaneous conversation should not take
long, perhaps five to ten minutes depending upon its intensity
and direction. The leader needs to be alert to the course of the
discussion. He calls the role-play to an abrupt halt, depending
on an impasse in the conversation, a significant statement just
uttered, or a petering out of comments.

When the pressure of the role-play is removed, the characters
are asked to review their principal arguments and determine
whether they have covered the situation. Then the audience is
invited to make observations and comments. The characters
may then be dismissed. This is the time for a general discus-

sion of the problem. The chalkboard can be used to list the many items for and against, and a concluding summary statement may be made by the discussion leader. This whole process may take from 30 to 45 minutes.

Many variables are possible. A word of warning must be noted, however, since role-playing is not suitable for every problem or question. Furthermore, there is a temptation to overuse role-playing. It is not the novelty of presentation, but the unique manner in which persons are cast in "some one else's shoes" that causes more profound thinking.

THE BUZZ SESSION

Another popular and widely-used technique is the *buzz-session*. Technically speaking, the buzz-session is a simultaneous discussion in little groups of six persons each, talking on one common question for only six minutes. There often comes a time in the course of a meeting that some issue becomes so exciting that everybody in the group wants to get a word in edgewise. Or the program leader may properly plan a buzz-session in advance as the means of total participation in dealing with the topic of the day.

To make the most effective use of a buzz-session, certain principles need to be observed. First, the question or topic to be discussed must be clearly stated, and should be of general interest. Such a question can be posed following the seeing of a film or listening to a major speech, in which case the question can be, "What does this film or speech say to our young people?" A group of young people may be confronted with, "What is our biggest problem in dealing with our parents?" or "What puzzles me most about being a Christian?"

Then the group must be divided into units of six to eight persons each. The ideal way is to count off the people so that those who came together or are sitting among friends will be divided, and therefore a new set of contacts can be established.

If, for instance, there are thirty persons in the room, count off by fives to get five groups of six persons each.

Immediately upon assembling at specially designated spots in the room (No. 1 meet in this corner, No. 2 by this table, or No. 1 under this light, No. 2 under this light), urge the groups to sit in close circles. In each group, let the members introduce each other and quickly agree on the chairman. The chairman's job is to see that the discussion goes around and around, putting the central question to each person. The group selects a recorder, who will keep a running commentary, and may then report to the total group.

Within the time limit of six minutes or so, every person in a group is given a chance to say his piece. Then by sharing the comments the group comes to agreement on their response by naming priorities. In fact, it may be necessary to limit each group to only one response, thus forcing the buzz-group to search for their best and most significant answer.

When the allotted time is up, the leader calls the whole discussion to a halt, and asks for reports which are listed on the chalkboard. It is entirely possible that there will be considerable duplication of answers. Enough basic thinking has been done in the buzz-groups so that members in the audience will now speak up more readily. The job at hand is to seek total group consent to the results on the board.

Both the role-play and the buzz-session are listed as valuable learning experiences because each of them involves a great number of persons. This does not imply, of course, that using either of these techniques will assure satisfactory learning, but it does open the way for deeper insight and greater understanding. The weakness is that in either case, the people may be seeking the "Sunday school answer" and may have covered up the more deep-seated and life-disturbing solutions. It then falls on the adult leader to call attention to the inadequate nature of the discussion and solution.

CHAPTER FOUR

The Place of Adults

YOUNG PEOPLE need the adult person for teaching, counseling, and guiding. His stability, experience, and perspective combine to make the adult worker a valuable and necessary person in the church's ministry to young people.

WHAT IS THE LEADER'S FUNCTION?

The idea of leadership is changing. The traditional concept of a leader is a person who dominates with authority and brilliance. He insists on his way, standing front and center, and does all the planning and thinking for his followers. This has been true of the "adult leader," either the church school teacher or the adult adviser to the fellowship group.

The new look indicates that leadership is not a person, but a function. Hence in a general discussion period, leadership shifts every time a different person speaks up. In committee work each person performs a different function, and assumes leadership in his task. While this may appear to invite confusion, the actual leadership has been transferred to the group, and the adult person—whether teacher or adviser—must review again his function and role.

For our discussion in this chapter, we will refer to the adult worker, who may be either or both teacher and adviser. In the formal setting of the morning church school class or in the informal fellowship meeting in the evening the role of the adult worker is generally the same. In fact, the desirable situation is for the same adult person to function both as teacher and adviser to the same group of young people. Let us consider some functions of the adult worker.

(1) *Understand the young people.* Perhaps an easier way to say this is, Let the adolescents understand themselves. With a little inquiry, you can find books, pamphlets, magazines, films, and filmstrips which help teenagers and adults understand the many complexities of growth. While much of this is written for the secular world, the factual information is usually sound. It becomes your duty to provide the spiritual significance in interpreting and evaluating the material. A valuable contribution of the church is to maintain a circulating library of this literature.

(2) *Remain adults among teenagers.* It would be wise to recognize that adult workers do not belong in the adolescent world. Adolescents should have their privacy. As adults, you would do well not to mimic them, and in fact, not become adolescents yourselves.

You might, however, be interested in their doings, and in their accomplishments. To go to school functions, whether it be a junior play, the football game, or the carnival, is to provide appreciation of the capacity and talent of young people. Note also who are doing the yeoman duty backstage. And in every instance, a word of recognition, a nod of encouragement, and a smile of congratulation will add to the sense of kinship. Follow the school paper, read the school annual, and welcome the opportunity to be a sponsor at a school dance. In addition to increasing your knowledge of them, you will be more respected for your interest in their accomplishments.

(3) *Provide opportunities.* A major function of the adult worker is to set the stage where the young people may be exposed to the Christian gospel and its implications. Whether in class or meeting, by speech or film, discussion or research, the

adult worker will help guide the young people into meaningful experiences.

(4) *Know the individuals in your group.* An important task for the adult worker is to know as much as possible about each person for whom he is responsible. A good suggestion is to keep a confidential card file or notebook of name, address, birth date, school grade, parents' name, parents' occupation, health, and church record. In addition, information on interests, hobbies, trips, activities, collections, and awards might be noted. Relations with girls or boys, achievements or accomplishments in school or community are also revealing. However, the significant notations are the week-to-week observations of a good job done in decorating, song leading, sign painting, or welcoming strangers. Perhaps on a certain subject, the young person showed considerable feeling or knowledge. The off-the-cuff remarks or attitudes make a helpful item to add to the record. Certainly, a direct question brought to the adult's attention, or a request for counseling, is to be entered.

This may be a time-consuming chore. But it helps us become alert to each individual and makes us better able to know what is behind outward behavior. It enables us to understand why some boy at 14 craves attention and needs the security of a steady girl friend. And if the record is carefully kept, it could be passed on to the new adult who takes over our responsibility.

(5) *Trust the group.* Our democratic culture provides all persons with some common education, and in spite of many doubts, our people are basically sound, good, and decent. It is thus that adult workers look upon teenagers and know that each of them has some brain power, a conscience, hopes and dreams, and a world of experiences. Out of their observations, travels, and research, our senior highs do conduct some basic discussions, arrive at earth-shaking decisions, and participate in pioneering projects.

There is of course that maxim of social workers, that we must begin with people "where they are." This means that some persons and some groups are more ready to embark upon a weekend spiritual retreat than others. Perhaps any group can enjoy a hayride, but only a few persons can write personal devotions for publication. But whatever the level of attainment, each person and each group can move on and up. In reverse, this says that we must enjoy our young people for what they are and not be impatient for what they are not.

(6) *Encourage free expression.* A more technical word is "permissive." The wise adult creates a pleasant and informal atmosphere, urges a relaxed and leisurely pursuit on a given subject, and encourages free expression of ideas. Because the adult worker has indicated his desire to learn with the young people, no question is brushed off, and all comments are received for consideration.

With such assurances, the teenagers will feel free to move into unexplored territory, express fears and doubts, and make shocking observations. There is no dirty look, the disapproving glance, or the slap on the wrist. Without appearing to take sides, the adult can show the opposite points of view with evaluation, and indicate his personal position on the subject.

There is real danger that the wrong decision (in the eyes of the adult) may be made, but this is the price we pay for democratic leadership.

(7) *Be alert to hidden needs.* Each person attends a meeting or class session for the purpose of studying, learning, or sharing in the fun or fellowship. This is the presumed reason why the class or meeting is held. Yet each individual comes out of a different situation, has different pressures on his life, seeks answers to different problems and is motivated differently from the rest of the group.

The adult worker is therefore in the delicate position of

watching for those hidden pressures and problems. Only as the class and group experiences help resolve the tensions and problems in the individual's life does church become meaningful. If shy Susie in the corner is making eyes at big Jim during the meeting this is a clue to understanding her behavior elsewhere.

(8) *Build group spirit.* Groupness is built by the "wanted" atmosphere, the essence of the redemptive fellowship. Every effort should be made to assure a sense of belonging, the feeling of being together, the importance of the group. The physical setting is helpful. Discard the straight rows of chairs and avoid the church pews if possible. If the group is not too large, sit around a large table. Sit in a tight circle, or a semi-circle. This might mean two or three concentric circles. Take out all the empty chairs and bring in chairs as latecomers arrive.

For the evening fellowship meeting, a time for informal socializing is desirable. Ice-breakers, folk songs, and light refreshments are helpful. If the group is still new, use name-badges for the first few meetings. This sense of groupness is particularly important in the teaching-learning situation because the best opportunities for learning happen in the interaction of people. Groupness is important also because people must immediately feel at home, significant, and useful in the few moments they are together.

Groupness is built by bringing the same people together under varying circumstances. A church school class can have fun at the teacher's house practicing for a play; the class can visit one of their sick classmates; all the members of the class can go skating, or swimming, or hayriding. Groupness is built by avoiding a division within the group, whether this is by permitting a few to dominate, or to decide an issue by a narrow majority vote. The group gets strength by talking things over, exploring both sides of the issue, and striving for group consent.

THE ADULT WORKER IN ACTION

The church school teacher appears to have one task, to teach the lesson Sunday after Sunday. While this is so, one needs to be somewhat critical of the teacher who makes himself a lecturer, depending upon his knowledge and adulthood to impress the lesson of the day upon teenage ears.

It would be strategic for this teacher to let the class know that he, too, has much to learn. In fact, when a new course is introduced, the teacher might page through the new material with the class members, and point up some of the highlights that are ahead, some new territory to explore, some inquiry and research that are necessary. Indeed, each new course brings a new hope of adventure that the teacher alone cannot assure. He invites the class members to share in the wonders of the trip ahead.

The young people will certainly have some reaction to the new material, ranging from complete indifference to eager pursuit. Assume that they have some knowledge and background on the subject matter. In general conversation, determine what lessons or areas appear more interesting, and what needs to be explored. Perhaps one or another of the class members may wish to make special research, or take a major assignment in preparation of one or more lessons. Encourage early participation by class members, involving as many as possible.

The lessons, then, become a group responsibility. The teacher, however, has a special role of resource person. He should not only read the lesson and the teacher's guidance material, but also make special effort to get background information on the course. This might mean extra reading, some films to see, some conference to attend, some questions to ask. He may ask some other adult persons in the church or community to join the class as additional resource persons, as occasion arises.

The teacher must be alert to the ways in which teaching and learning take place. Depending upon space, time, and facilities, the class procedure can be varied and mysterious. This, too, might mean the reading of some helpful books and articles in current magazines for church school teachers, both of one's own denomination and of the National Council of Churches.

Certainly the teacher must have some basic knowledge of adolescent young people, and especially of that age-group with which he meets. Frequent reading on this subject from books, pamphlets, and magazines is helpful. In addition, the teacher ought to know each pupil personally.

This suggests that the teacher should find occasion to see his pupils outside the regular Sunday morning class period. It is for this reason that the teacher should know what the evening youth fellowship program is, and cooperate with the adult advisers of the evening group. It is desirable that the teacher share occasionally in the fellowship program, and thereby be identified with a wider aspect of the church's ministry. Some first-hand knowledge of home and school life will also be valuable.

Thus, the teacher is expected to know the material, the teaching techniques, adolescent youth, and the individual pupils. His is the teaching responsibility of the local church in the formal and systematic study of the course for that class.

Because the evening fellowship group usually deals with the same persons as the morning classes, some churches provide a continuity of adult leadership as well as unity in experience. Hence there may be a direct relationship between the morning class lesson and the evening fellowship topic.

In some churches there are evening fellowship groups which operate independently of the morning church school experience, and select their topics on the basis of their own interests and inclinations. There is a third group of churches which provide "dated" topics for evening meetings. In any event, there is an air of informality about the evening groups which affects the role and function of the adult adviser.

He must play the middle course between the mother-hen baby-sitter type who sits in the back row to keep the group from getting out of hand, and the dominating dictator type who sits in the front and controls with an iron fist. The adviser recognizes that this is a youth group, which must itself determine the direction and speed with which it moves. Some youth groups resent adult interference, and the adult person knows that he must be careful not to tread where he is not wanted.

On the other hand, while young people are anxious to run their own program, they know they need the restraining hand, the wisdom and advice of adult persons, and an occasional suggestion and stimulation. Young people want to be praised, but they also know when they deserve a scolding.

Most important, the adult worker must consistently fill the role of counselor. He must have a definite, but indirect, influence in all the decisions that are being made. He should add his mature judgment, and especially a Christian influence, in the activities and projects that go on. In the discussion period, the adult person must be careful to stay apart, and to speak only when asked. He may make an observation from time to time, to correct misinterpretation, or to bring the conversation into proper perspective. He may ask for the privilege of summarizing the discussions. But always he takes the position of an invited guest. This is a delicate but necessary balance.

From week to week, the adult worker is teaching his young people how to make decisions, how to prepare the topic presentation, what is desirable in worship experiences, where to find the best recreational suggestions, who can give the best answers to religious questions and other questions that come up. In his quiet way, the adult person keeps his pulse on groupness, gives sturdiness to the group, and watches for the stray individual who slips out of the group life. The adult worker must develop his technique in dealing with young people, and know the individuals in his group. But probably most important, he must make a conscious effort to increase his spiritual grasp, his understanding of the Christian faith, and his commitment to God and the church.

Consider, then, the many roles of the adult worker with youth:

(1) An example of a mature Christian adult

(2) A counselor to whom young people turn with personal problems

(3) A middle-man to speak for youth interests before the congregational boards and committees

(4) A stimulator of the group process, in discussing, planning, and deciding

(5) A coach, who teaches, inspires, scolds, praises and demonstrates

(6) A resource person, who has done previous or simultaneous study of the lesson or topic, and perhaps additional study, to suggest answers and solutions in the class and meeting

(7) An observer who notes the acceptance or rejection of a lonely person, the progress of the group spirit, the maintenance of the Christian standard

(8) An arbitrator, who may be invited to settle differences of fact, opinion, or judgment

(9) A coordinator who double-checks all preparations and arrangements for regular and special activities of the youth group

(10) A disciplinarian, who quietly but deliberately insists on punctuality, order and respect, in class and meeting sessions

DESIRABLE ATTRIBUTES

From these descriptions it appears that the church and the young people have high expectations of the adult worker. Indeed, this is so. Yet we recognize that there is no angelic figure who answers all the noble requirements. But for those adult persons who would like to have a few pointers on what young people desire in them, here are some observations.

(1) *The adult worker with young people must have status in the church.* That is to say, the teacher or adviser must be properly related to the life of the church, officially appointed or assigned, with the full authority of the congregation to serve in the youth program.

(2) *He must be impartial, neutral, and fair in dealing with the young people.* Any favoritism which may be expressed in any way will soon be detected, and the adult worker will lose influence and the respect of his young people. It is at this point that parents of teenagers have a delicate task as leaders.

(3) *He must exhibit signs of sincerity, warmth, patience, and understanding in working with the changeable and unpredictable young people.* While teenagers appear to reject adult authority, they seek desperately for the help and guidance of the friendly adult.

(4) On the other hand, the *adult leader must reflect stability, with some firm convictions of his own, high ideals and standards, and basic objectives for working with the growing adolescents.* For this, he must lay down some rules, be firm in defining limits, and demonstrate disciplinary powers. Similarly, he is quick to praise and makes special effort to congratulate the individual or the group for a task well done.

(5) *He must reveal faith and love, a trusting spirit.* Optimism and assurance mark his attitude as young people plan and dream. He deliberately and consciously lifts the vision and hope of the teenagers to live more meaningful lives, to have better relationships with people, to gain spiritual depth and insight.

(6) *The adult worker acknowledges the inadequacy of his grasp of Christian beliefs, his knowledge of the subject matter to teach or lead, of methods and resources, his understanding of*

young people. But because of this, he makes an effort to improve his knowledge by reading, observing, experimenting, and exposing himself to learning situations. He prays for divine guidance, seeks help from the Bible, and confers with his minister.

(7) *He tries to build the group spirit.* It is not his task to make young people loyal to him, to depend upon him, and to revere him. On the contrary, his task is to strengthen the group unity, to make young people more self-reliant, help them to become more mature under his guidance. He helps the group to become sensitive to the needs of those individuals who are not being won by the group.

(8) *The young people will normally expect the adult worker to be dependable.* While teenagers may themselves shirk responsibility, they will not forgive their adult worker for being late, for inadequate preparation, or unexcused absences. This means that adults must be prepared to give considerable time to young people.

(9) *He must always be identified as an adult, though he is surrounded by teenagers.* While acting and behaving as an adult person, he should participate in the youth activities, and share enthusiastically in their interests, within reason.

(10) *As for age and marital status,* we feel that *the effectiveness of the adult lies in his attitude and spirit.* It is true, nevertheless, that teenage young people are more apt to confide in those who are not too far removed from their own age. Yet the worker must be removed enough to have weathered a few storms and to have had his faith tested. The adult worker who is from five to ten years older than his young people often becomes the "hero." His words and views are more welcome, since he probably "understands" teenagers better. And for well-rounded guidance, a man and woman combination, or man-

and-wife team appears desirable to cope with the boy-girl situations in teenage strife.

(11) *The adult worker's relationship with the parents of his young people poses a dilemma.* Because the teenagers are in the stage of rebelling against their parents, any indication of close identification with parents may tend to lose the confidence of the young people. This is especially so if the young people suspect their parents of "using" the adult worker to mold young people to parental desires. On the other hand, the adult worker must be on speaking terms with the parents and have their confidence and trust. A knowledge of the parents and the family of a young person is essential in understanding him.

(12) *The adult worker becomes the symbol of the youth program in the eyes of the congregation.* He must defend the young people, interpret the program, secure funds and facilities for them, represent them before the official church bodies, and secure adult cooperation for youth activities.

(13) Finally, *the adult person is willing to have his life touched and changed by the discipline and experience of Christian fellowship.* He prays that such challenge will take place in the lives of his young people. No adult worker can stand outside the activities he provides for the young people. He too is involved to the hilt.

HOW SECURE ADULT WORKERS?

The recruitment of lay adult workers to serve as teachers and advisers to young people is a serious and important task. The committee or board of Christian education of the local congregation, together with the minister, is probably the best group to give thorough study to this matter. Such a committee is always on the alert for prospective church school teachers. The minister knows the availability, background, and personality of possible recruits for working with young people. The young people themselves, or at least the youth officers, should share in the consideration of the new appointment.

In considering possible lay workers, the following factors should be reviewed:

(1) They ought not be already too involved in church responsibilities.

(2) They have indicated some interest in working with young people, or in the life of the church.

(3) They seem willing to learn, eager to be of service.

(4) They have a good spirit, a sense of churchmanship.

(5) They would probably react favorably to the difficult challenge.

When all possible names have thus been reviewed and the first and alternate selections named for the immediate vacancies, the appointment is officially authorized.

The minister of the church, with a representative youth officer, then brings the news to the selected person or couple. The process of selection assures the new leaders that they are acceptable to the young people, to the minister, and to the church organization responsible for youth work. The minister assures them that they will be relieved of other obligations they may now hold in the life of the congregation so that they can concentrate on the youth program. The minister also assures them of budget, manpower, and facilities, of the cooperation of the congregation and the church organizations. The minister also indicates that they should explore every opportunity for leadership training.

The youth representative assures them of the young people's desire to have their adult guidance, interprets some of the present youth activities, and asks that they accept this assignment.

This invitation may come as a surprise and an immediate answer need not be expected. It is true, however, that a "call" of this type, carrying the weight and impact of the young people, the minister, and the official church body, cannot easily be set aside. It is important that this process should not appear mechanical; it should be clear that those who are invited have been selected after prayers seeking the guidance of God.

While many churches ordinarily extend an invitation of this type for a one-year term, a longer commitment of perhaps three or five years would be desirable. This gives adult workers an opportunity to become well versed in the field, to provide continuity of leadership, and to become acquainted with the young people. After considerable experience they can also give more valuable guidance to those who come after them.

Upon receiving their acceptance, the new adult workers will be related to the Christian education program of the church, and make regular reports to the responsible committee or board. At the appropriate time, they will be publicly consecrated or commissioned for their task.

Another source of adult workers is the committee on youth work of the local congregation. Such a committee may be formed by parents, the teachers in the youth division, scout leaders and other adults who work with teenagers in the church, and a representative of the women's or men's group whose task is to undergird the youth program. This committee gives general supervision to all phases of the church's ministry to young people.

Thus one of the functions of this committee on youth work is to provide adult teachers and advisers. Committee members themselves may assume special assignments to look after personnel, worship and recreation leadership, library and other resources, finances and facilities, transportation and food, public relations and youth integration in the life of the congregation.

This team approach makes a regular and systematic process of training and securing adult workers to fill vacancies. The correlation of activities, the extension into new experience, and the adjustment to changing teenage population can be properly done by this committee.

OTHER ADULTS IN THE CHURCH

There are other adults in the congregation who have direct relationship to the youth program of the church.

(1) *The Minister.* The minister stands in the unique position of being the spiritual shepherd of his flock, of ministering to all members, of preaching the gospel, of coordinating the many activities and organizations in the church, and of extending the Christian influence into the life of the community.

His relationship to the youth program, then, is principally as resource person, bringing specialized knowledge and skill, sharing in significant experiences and activities, and insisting that the youth program be consistent with the total program of the church. He should not be burdened with the details of running youth meetings, of double-checking arrangements and preparation, of collecting funds and equipment, of chauffeuring people to meetings, of mimeographing programs and telephoning for last-minute replacements. These are functions that other persons can and ought to do, thus relieving the minister for his other responsibilities.

(2) *Director of Christian Education.* There are churches which employ professional help to assist the minister. Such persons may be ordained ministers who serve as assistant or associate ministers, with special responsibility for the youth program. Others may be trained directors of Christian education, who list the youth program among other duties. Some few churches also have full-time or part-time directors of youth work, trained or untrained. There are churches which engage students from seminaries or colleges on weekends to teach a church school class, or to work with the youth fellowship group.

Because of their special skill and their professional status, these leaders have unusual opportunities to provide a significant youth program. They have first-hand contact with resources, their grasp of Christian foundations is more firm, theirs is a long-term dedication to the Christian education task. It would normally be expected that youth programs under such guidance should be superior to those under lay leadership.

However, the church which provides such professional leadership may find that the lay adults of the church tend to shirk their responsibility, expecting the paid personnel to carry all the burden of the program. In such instances, the lay members of the church feel insulted and imposed upon when they are asked to give of their time and services. It is essential, then, that the role of these professional persons be clearly described at the outset.

For instance, whether the minister or other professional leaders are interested in the youth program, the basic responsibility should rest first in the appropriate board or committee on Christian education, who then assign the task to a lay adult person or couple. The professional leaders should be in a position to help the lay adult teachers and advisers, providing suggestions, strengthening their techniques, demonstrating new resources, and encouraging their efforts. By agreement, certain specialized assignments may be taken by the professional leader, but his best role is to be the resource person.

(3) *Club Leaders.* The active church usually sponsors scout units for boys and girls of several ages. In the youth age, the adult leaders of the Boy Scout and the Girl Scout troops often work with the same young people who are in church school class and youth fellowship group. There are also youth choirs, dramatics, athletics, hobbies, and craft. There can also be other church-related agencies like the Y.M.C.A., Y.W.C.A., and

Camp Fire Girls, who may use church facilities, or be sponsored by the church, or involve church young people.

Where there is no committee on youth work, all leaders, teachers, and advisers who carry some responsibility to the teenage young people should meet together periodically and review their total work. They may consider schedules, emphases, facilities, finances, and cooperative ventures. A quarterly meeting of this group is recommended, so that a common ministry to young people can be realized.

(4) *Superintendent of the Youth Division.* There are churches which appoint or assign a lay adult person to be superintendent of the youth division in the church school, or a director or chairman of youth work for all youth functions, both church school and youth fellowship. These non-professional leaders have the task of coordinating the many activities involving young people, providing leadership training opportunities, necessary resource material and literature, and interpreting the youth program to higher church bodies.

(5) *Church Officials.* Members and officers of the top responsible body of the congregation should be remembered in planning the youth program. A sympathetic, friendly group of men and women will certainly be a blessing. But there are churches whose church "fathers" are opposed to youth functions and deny funds, facilities, and privileges. Special efforts to cultivate these people are in order.

(6) *Adult Members.* Adult members of the congregation may or may not be aware of the fine work being done with the young people of the church. It is not necessary that public attention be called to the youth program at all times. However, a fair and adequate report of the youth program may be made through the parish paper, annual meetings, and church bulletins. An occasional all-church affair, involving the young people in some distinctive manner, may be helpful.

(7) *Parents.* The parents of your teenagers should certainly be interested in your program. One way to bring them in is to arrange for a "parents of the month" series, inviting one set of parents to share in the evening youth program, providing transportation when necessary, serving refreshments on occasion, opening their home or other facilities for small-group meetings, and in general, observing the activities of their young people. A new set of parents can be involved each month.

Similarly, one set of parents can be invited on rotation one Sunday each month to sit and observe the church school class in session. It is also possible to invite some parents to make presentations of varying kinds, depending upon their special field, on the lesson or topic under discussion.

This raises another question. Can parents of a teenager be teachers and advisers of young people? From the teenager's point of view, it would be most uncomfortable and unnatural to have his parents serve as teacher or adviser. Because objectivity and equal treatment are especially necessary in the adult worker, the parent will find difficulty in dealing fairly with his child in a youth class or group. Family relationships and tensions may be exposed and embarrass all concerned.

(8) *Older Adults.* The alert church also has, either organized or unorganized, an older adult group. These persons, when physically able, are often willing to provide refreshments, cook meals, bake, or prepare covered dishes for youth functions. Such interest should definitely be cultivated. In return, the young people can make a special effort to seek out and visit shut-ins and the disabled in this group. For a young person to "adopt a grandparent" in this manner has proved satisfying and rewarding.

CHAPTER FIVE

The Balanced Youth Program

YOUNG PEOPLE need constant awareness of the presence of God. While secular activities and material abundance surround the teenager's daily life, the sense of humility and devotion must be cultivated and learned. Hence, our young people need a sense of communication with God, and a real understanding of Christian worship.

The first requirement is diligent and faithful attendance at the regular Sunday morning worship. There should be no apology for this insistence. In fact, the whole atmosphere of the local church should take for granted that every teenager should be present in this central act of all Christian witness. There is, in truth, a heavy burden on the minister to speak to these adolescent members in the pews, and to involve them in the service as ushers, choir members, and occasionally as liturgists. But above all, it is essential that every young person in your church establish this pattern and habit of regular Sunday morning attendance at church worship.

There is also the period of worship during the church school hour. Depending on the tradition and custom of the local church, this can vary from a brief, meaningful period of devotion, to a lengthy session of hymn singing, announcements, and the superintendent's story. It is hardly necessary to point out that to too many persons, this may be the only corporate worship experience in the week. Whether this is so or not, the responsibility of the church ministry is to make the moment of church school worship as profound and sacred as possible. Here, too, participation and leadership in the worship by young people, as individuals or as classes, can lift the sights and insights of teenagers in the worship experience.

In the evening youth fellowship meeting, the conduct of worship is rightly regarded as a youth responsibility. With adult guidance and counsel in planning, the actual presentation of prayers, Scripture reading, brief meditation, and other elements of the devotional service should be by young people. This experience gives better understanding, increased confidence, and new appreciation of worship.

However, the young people quite honestly do not know what to expect in a worship experience, nor do they realize what constitutes worship. On the surface, they are aware that a few hymns, some scripture verses, a prayer, a poem, perhaps an offering, and the meditation message, constitute the devotions. This is so easily thrown together, that young people in charge of the worship period can often be found flipping through the pages of the hymnal a few moments before the meeting opens. It is here that the adult adviser and the minister can give valuable guidance.

First and foremost, it is highly desirable that the worship moments carry a theme, through the hymns, Scripture, and other elements of the service. This theme should be related to the topic discussion to follow, or some other experience in store for the young people.

Next, it follows that preparation should be adequate and thoughtful. The knowledge of the use of hymns, the selection of Scripture, the use of resource material—whether it be a story, meditation, poem, a short film, filmstrip, or a picture—should be carefully taught. The pianist might need to practice beforehand. The reader of Scripture can use some preliminary exercises to get used to words and names.

Probably a neglected aspect of worship is the atmosphere in

which this period is observed. One youth group learned in a summer church camp that in approaching vesper point the young people become silent when they pass the "gates," and remain silent throughout the service and until they pass these same "gates" at the end of the service. Thereupon these young people adopted the same practice. They now gather in another room or hallway before entering the worship room, where they maintain dignified quiet during the service, except, of course, where audience participation is involved.

What is done about the worship center, the arrangement of chairs, the effective use of lighting, and the musical prelude can add depth and meaning to worship. Whether to have a worship leader or not, whether to sing with or without accompaniment, whether to sit in straight rows or in a circle, whether to use candles or flowers—these can be given due consideration from time to time.

Young people must learn the difference between hymns and other music with religious themes. From time to time, a popular song of the day with religious overtones becomes the rage. Young people may sing it as part of a worship experience, not realizing how inaccurately and inadequately the words express their theology. Again, there are songs which go over big in a fellowship song session, but do not make for worshipful singing. An honest appraisal and study of this subject is a helpful exercise.

The inclusion of a worship talk of any length in a youth meeting is not recommended. This assumes, of course, that the whole evening meeting is not considered a "devotional meeting" which necessitates an "inspirational message" of some kind. In a youth meeting the period of devotion, whether at the beginning or at the end of the evening program, should be brief and concise, keeping separate the much more informal topic and discussion period, and the fellowship hour. Readings and poems must be used carefully, guarding against sentimental gush.

After all is said and done, these remarks point only to the external makings of the worship program. Of more importance than place, form, and sequence is the attitude of worship, the conversation with God, and the anticipation of divine presence. Teenagers must learn and relearn the true sense of worship. Here are some observations on a recommended order:

(1) *Call to Worship*. In the language of the Bible, an appropriate verse can be uttered or read. This is the declaration that God is present.

(2) *Hymn of Praise and Adoration*. The worshipers respond to the presence by a joyous hymn of praise. This is not the time to use hymns which focus on "I," but on God.

(3) *Prayer of Confession*. The worshipers continue their response by a prayer stating in simple and honest terms their unworthiness and failure as God's children. Such a prayer can be freely given, or can be read by the group. Traditional prayers of confession may be used.

(4) *God's Word*. God speaks now through the words of the Bible. The scripture lesson sets forth a message which speaks to the young people. Appropriate selections should be carefully made. The meditation or sermon when given later is considered an extension of the scripture lesson.

(5) *Hymn and Creed*. In response to God's word, the worshipers sing a hymn of faith, consecration, or service. At this time, a vigorous spirit of personal devotion is expressed. For this reason, the Apostle's Creed may be properly used as a unison statement.

(6) *Fellowship of Prayer*. In further response to God's word in Scripture, prayer is given. Prayers of intercession and supplication are best at this point. Intercession is prayer offered for others; supplication is prayer for personal needs. These may be free prayers offered by the leader or by several persons. Again, the rich treasury of traditional prayers provides good

suggestions. The Lord's Prayer, and a period of directed silent prayers may also be used.

(7) *The Blessing.* The benediction is God's promise to be with the worshipers, to surround them with his love and care. The leader accepts this promise in behalf of the group.

This brief outline suggests the essential steps for a meaningful worship. It allows for the use of hymns, Scripture, and prayer to suit the evening's program. Your minister can give further guidance and instruction on this subject.

Beyond the experiences of group or corporate worship, the young people need to develop the practice of personal devotions. By setting aside a few moments each day in the privacy of one's room, using guidance material to stimulate one's thoughts, a young person finds new insight and spiritual strength. Here is opportunity for daily Bible reading, the brief moment of prayer, and reflective thinking. The problems and tensions of the day can be seen in perspective, and new directions for daily living may be made clear. Young people who attend summer camps and conferences speak warmly of this morning watch experience.

The principal value of personal devotion is the discipline which requires the teenager to pause in his daily schedule, at a regular time in the early morning or before retiring. This discipline becomes part of his normal life, and increase his sense of worship and reverence of God.

Your denomination provides or recommends daily devotional material suitable for young people. Discuss the possibilities in church school class and youth fellowship meeting. Get the total group to commit each member for a one-month period. Review and evaluate the experience, urging continued observance.

STUDY

Moments of concentrated study contribute to the development of the mature Christian person. Without question, the Sunday church school should have regular classes, separate for junior high and senior high pupils, with competent teachers and adequate facilities. Here again is the insistent necessity that your church provide periods of study of the Christian gospel, the life and teachings of Jesus Christ, the message of the prophets, an understanding of Paul and his ministry, the history and heritage of the Protestant church and of your denomination, the responsibility of Christians in the social order, an understanding of growing persons, God's magnificence revealed in nature, and God's ever-present love for and judgment upon mankind.

Responsible Christian educators in your denomination have given thoughtful consideration to the preparation and distribution of suitable church school material for the several age-groupings of your church. We urge your use of your denominationally-recommended literature because it more properly teaches your young people the theology acceptable to your church, provides a progressive and comprehensive program through the years, maintains sound educational and psychological principles, and includes pertinent and significant contributions of your denomination to the life-stream of Protestantism.

As every teenager should be led to participate regularly in the Sunday morning worship service, so every teenager should be expected to attend his appropriate church school class, and provision should be made to receive every such person.

Another opportunity for Christian study comes in the discussion of topics in the evening fellowship meetings. Whereas the church school material is arranged systematically and usually taught by adults, the evening meetings usually provide a completely free and varied choice of subject matter, wholly dependent upon the interests and inclinations of the young people themselves.

In these evening meetings, the young people can explore further the problems and pressures that bear on their lives, and seek the Christian implications and answers. The topics can range from the most personal boy-girl concerns to the general issue of war and peace. To help these young people wrestle adequately with any of their chosen topics, your denomination provides an array of resource materials including suggestions for topics, film, drama, study books, and articles in magazines. Whether the topic materials are dated or undated, they can become a cumulative library of information to be used as problems arise.

Using undated material might indicate a haphazard system of securing topics for discussion, but most youth fellowship groups try to provide for order as well as spontaneity. One method is to map out a long-term program by finding out what topics and subjects seems to be of current interest to the members of the group. This can be done by a period of relaxed discussion, or through the use of an interest-finder questionnaire. Another way would be to browse through the program resource book or magazine provided by the denomination, and secure indications of interest on each topic. A third way would be to leave the choice of topics to the several committees or commissions which carry program area responsibilities.

In addition to the church school and evening fellowship groups, most churches provide some sort of confirmation instruction or church membership classes for young teenagers. Though the actual age and practice may vary from church to church, the young teenager definitely needs specific instructions to prepare him for membership in the congregation. This study venture can be a major contribution to his grasp of the Christian faith and his responsibility as a churchman.

There are youth groups which have made efforts to provide study experiences beyond the opportunities listed above. One denomination has adopted the plan of recommending a reading book of the year, and provides a paper-bound reading book each year for the Lenten season. Some churches invite the young people to a special Lenten study series. Bible study in an informal atmosphere during week-nights flourishes here and there. And those churches which provide a reading table or circulating library of pamphlets, booklets, and books of interest to young people are making a helpful contribution to youth development.

SERVICE

One test of the true Christian is to observe the extent, manner and motive of his giving, whether it be money, time, or talent. A group of young people may have been on the receiving end of the church ministry for so long that they have not realized that theirs is also a giving responsibility.

Acting as individuals or as a group, the young people are capable of making a sizable contribution to the life of the church, community, or nation through gifts of hours, strength, and work. Undergirding this whole aspect is a spirit of consecration and devotion, of willingness to serve others in the name of the church and of Christ, and in true stewardship of the strength and abilities given them by God.

While we do not pretend to present a total list of service projects which young people have done and can do, we group them and describe some to indicate possibilities.

(1) *Service to the Minister and the Church.* Young people can do any number of routine office tasks like typing or mimeographing, stuffing envelopes or delivering notes, making minor repairs to furniture or building, doing landscaping or special house cleaning, running errands, providing needed manpower on call, and putting out a monthly newssheet.

(2) *Service to Church Worship.* On occasion young people can usher, greet, pass out or collect hymnals, help in the liturgy, sing in the choir, serve as acolyte.

(3) *Service to Church Organizations and Members.* Young people can wait on table and do dishes at suppers, visit shut-ins, go caroling, assist in vacation church school, have a story hour for young children on Saturdays, present a play or participate

in Christmas or Easter observances, serve the Easter breakfast, welcome new teenage church members at a special reception or banquet, baby-sit for church school teachers.

(4) *Service to Community.* Young people have cleaned cemeteries, cleared vacant lots and converted them to play areas, received clothing for relief, worked in clothing centers for overseas shipment, entertained and visited hospitals, children's homes, and old people's homes. Imaginative groups have planted trees, clamored for an adequate teenage recreation center, attempted to correct cheating and drinking in school, secured a foreign exchange student, entered a float in the community parade.

Specific opportunities vary from community to community and from church to church, but every youth group should be alert to some service experience during the year. In doing these service tasks, one word of caution must be stressed: in no event should public notice be the motivation of such work. True Christian humility insists that our good deeds be kept quiet.

Another area of youth service is a new and growing realm of voluntary work. On a purely local basis, the common expression of voluntary service can be a day of work by the total membership of a certain youth group gleaning corn, clearing a camp ground, or providing leadership at a recreation center. It could be a weekend work-camp, where groups of young people come from several churches and in a deteriorating neighborhood do some plastering, wallpapering, and painting. It could be young people who give most of their summer weeks for camp counseling, for caravaning or work-camping. And for a few, this can mean a whole summer or more in a work-camp sponsored by the Commission on Ecumenical Voluntary Service Projects in this country or abroad.

The newest of these voluntary service projects is the one-year service program sponsored by at least two denominations.

Coming first for two months' training, a one-year volunteer is then sent to a mission station, benevolent institution, or other church-related agency for a ten-month period. A new group is trained each quarter.

The philosophy which underlies most of these service programs insists that Christian love and concern be the motivation. In the actual work, work-campers and caravaners are expected to identify themselves with the people they serve, and do not set themselves apart in any way. A definite routine for these volunteers includes time for study, devotions, recreation, and cultural improvement. And in most instances, work-campers are expected to pay their own expenses of travel and maintenance. The languages of pick and shovel, of work and worship, of varying background of language, race and custom all blend in a Christian community of understanding and love.

A more common expression of Christian service is in the concern for the missionary outreach of your church. Two principal ways are noted: mission study and financial gifts. Youth leaders should know that twenty-eight denominations are cooperating through the Commission on Missionary Education where denominational representatives come together and agree on annual emphasis themes for both the home and the foreign fields and publish books under the trade name of Friendship Press.

The three age-group committees—children, youth, and adult —begin the task of outlining suitable books, audio-visuals, maps, drama, and other materials for the many age-groups in our churches. For our particular concern, we need to know that every year a new set of material is available on the home mission theme, and another set for the foreign mission theme, and that these are written for junior highs, and another batch for senior highs, and sometimes another for college students. Your denominational representatives are involved in every step of the development, from the creation of the themes to the finished products. The likelihood is that for several years now, you have been using these Friendship Press materials in some way or another.

In addition to the Friendship Press material, your denominational missionary enterprise requires special study. In every instance, the purpose of the youth fellowship group is to share in bringing the gospel and the Christian witness to non-Christians, within our national borders and beyond. Thus, some basic and serious study on the missionary task is essential.

The other aspect of this concern is the giving of financial support to undergird these missionary activities. Most denominational youth programs have a comprehensive plan to coordinate missionary study and financial giving. These plans may carry such names as the Youth Fund, Benevolent Goal, World Service Fund, Youth Budget, Dedicated Dollars, Sharing Plan, World Friendship Fund, and Youth Offering Project. While the details of money-giving vary in each of these programs, the philosophy is usually quite similar. Young people are encouraged to study certain mission areas and give, either directly to projects designated for the year, or to the total missionary program.

In addition to the financial support of the missionary work of your own denomination, your youth group may be participating in an international, interdenominational program known as World Youth Projects, sponsored by the Youth Department of the World Council of Churches and the World Council of Christian Education. Through World Youth Projects, Christian youth around the world strengthen Christian fellowship by supporting each other's work and program. Thus your denomination may have selected a project in Asia or Africa or elsewhere for a given year, while a Christian youth group in Europe might support some work in the United States or in Asia. Watch for the World Youth Project as you plan your missionary giving.

The matter of money in the youth program requires evaluation. Young people have been known to raise money by submitting a float for a parade, by sponsoring a booth at a fair, by cake sale, ice cream social, talent show, skating party, May fair, supper, rummage sale, collecting scrap and waste paper, and countless other ways. They have raised varying sums from $15 to $400 by these activities. With money thus accumulated they have given to their church building fund, organ fund, carpet fund, and parsonage fund. They have purchased outdoor bulletin boards, mimeograph machines, projection equipment, coffee urns, and other sundry pieces of furniture for the church. They have given to their missionary projects, and financed their summer excursions. They have established camp scholarships. Indeed, when it comes to raising and handling money, young people are quite adept and independent.

Many youth groups look with considerable pride on achievements and their contributions. It is certainly true that in the cooperative efforts for earning and raising these funds, the young people had a good time. In some instances, they were prevailed upon by the adult members of the church to accept a "challenge" toward the financial program of the moment.

We look with doubtful eyes at these money-raising activities. The energies of a youth group should be directed toward study and service, for experiences which enrich their knowledge and attitudes. The basic purpose of the youth program needs to be lifted and seen anew. We question the wisdom of using competitive tactics in raising money, and of making the special gift as a matter of pride. One youth group had a balance of $400 in a bank account, and the group slowly withered away while it sought to protect that amount. It is a tragic commentary of the day for a youth group to be renowned for its bank balance or its ability to make certain gifts from time to time.

The alternative then is to abolish the youth group's treasury. Permit no bank balance, no bank account. Insist that young people be responsible members of the congregation by assuming reasonable weekly pledges. When there are campaigns for special funds, let each person make his personal pledge and gift. Funds which are raised in group activity, such as the earnings from Christ's Workday*, are to be given away promptly and completely through established congregational channels.

In return, the young people should request and receive an adequate and appropriate share of the congregational budget. Whether the annual sum is $50 or $200 will depend upon the needs and the program. Such items as these ought surely to be provided for: program resource books, films, honoraria for speakers, obligations to regional and national youth fellowship organizations, library and recreational supplies, travel expenses to conferences and institutes. List each of these with other items that you feel necessary and a proposed amount for each item. Total the list, and submit this budget before the congregation reviews its annual program. This procedure may take time to establish, but the practice is recommended.

For food at occasional suppers and the light refreshments for the evening meetings, do not use the budgeted funds. Depend on a "pay-as-you-go" basis. Thus, for instance, a fair charge can be made for a supper meal; donations can usually cover the refreshments. Some system of rotation among members and parents may be arranged so that refreshment costs can be shared.

If the young people enjoy the ice cream social, the talent show, and other valid money-makers, insist that every dollar earned be given to the congregational treasurer without comment or murmur. Similarly, for any legitimate major expense required by the youth program, a proper request should be presented and considered by the appropriate church body. In any event, give consideration to the pattern suggested by your denominational youth program.

---

*See chapter 8 for description of Christ's Workday.

RECREATION

Play and fun in the lives of young people are to be encouraged. Certainly the church should provide facilities, leadership, and opportunity for frequent and varied expressions of social good times. Such play-time need not always be for the sheer joy of companionship and recreation. All the creative aptitudes of the teenagers can be corraled in dramatic efforts, in crafts, music, and the arts.

(1) *Social Time in the Youth Meetings.* Every youth fellowship meeting should provide some time for a period of games and fun. We would divide the fun-time into two: informal pre-meeting activities, and group recreation.

On the basis that the meeting starts when the first person arrives, it is a good practice to encourage your young people to come a full half-hour before the meeting time. Anticipate also the presence of one or two newcomers at each meeting. Be certain that those in charge are on hand to secure participation in the informal activities.

Coming from different homes and experiences, a group of young people need to become acclimated to the youth meeting situation, and especially to each other. The feeling of strangeness must be replaced with the sense of belonging. Some physical activity in the beginning draws people out of their self-consciousness. Because people drift in from time to time, it is not fair to penalize the early-comers, nor to delay the meeting for the late-comers. Anticipate this awkward moment by providing for the pre-meeting activities.

During this pre-meeting time, ping-pong, shuffleboard, checkers, and other board games can absorb people as they come. A reading table of pamphlets and books may be helpful. A bulletin board with the latest significant articles, cartoons, and notes can be a useful eye-catcher. Perhaps you might try previewing some film or filmstrip, asking the early ones to make critical observations. Gathering around the piano for impromptu singing is good. Any or all of these can be going on at the same time. Occasionally this informal period might lead into an organized ice-breaker or mixer period.

Besides having most of the people assembled to start the regular part of the meeting on time, this informal session allows your teenagers a chance to visit each other.

(2) *The Recreation Period.* A desirable practice is to allow some time in each youth fellowship meeting for organized group recreation. Such a period should be considered part of the total evening program, and not an optional if-you-want-to session. This is also not the time for do-what-you-want activities such as those suggested for the pre-meeting period. The group recreation period can be at the beginning, middle, or end of the evening meeting. This helps establish the sense of groupness in fun. Every person, including the adults, should be expected to join in.

Whether the group is large or small, the youth leaders in charge must make adequate preparation for a full and varied program. Though adult help in planning is recommended, the actual preparation and leadership should be done by two or more young people for each meeting. Thus youth leadership may rotate for each meeting, or for a series of meetings, depending on the over-all pattern for sharing responsibility. One or two youth persons should be designated as recreation coordinator to maintain standards, and watch over the resource equipment.

A basic library of recreational books should be available. In addition, a scrapbook or card file of new games and activities can be kept. Some phonograph records and a good record player will be useful for folk games and square dancing. Space for recreational activities and storage space for supplies and equipment are also desirable.

Now as to the actual games and activities—your young people

have a wealth of resources from which to choose. These include a storehouse of fellowship and folk songs; quiet and sitting games; singing, running and relay games; traditional board games, musical games, folk dances, square dances, and games using balls or other apparatus.

If the first rule of good recreational leadership is adequate preparation, the second rule is good progression of activities. Progression calls for a sequence of games, usually starting with some quiet all-group mixers or songs, moving to active games or dances; then to some quiet sitting games; again into the active running games; then perhaps to refreshments and group singing and to a quiet relaxed closing fellowship circle.

To secure this pattern, your youth leaders must get a fair grasp of the many possible activities, with substitute activities to replace or adjust the prepared program. They must be flexible enough to cut short or to extend, and alert to the mood of the group. This comes, of course, with practice and experience. But all these fine details are necessary to lift the level of this social period in the youth fellowship meeting.

It is highly essential that refreshments be served as part of the recreational program, so that the group may have a formal closing. To permit the meeting to break apart without a definite closing service is most undesirable.

(3) *The Big Party.* A major social function several times a year adds spice to the youth program. Often the local community and its facilities will determine the nature and extent of these activities, but the usual ones include hayrides, skating, swimming, picnics, campfires, excursions, and the like. There are also planned parties during the year built around the holiday themes. Your recreation library can provide many suggestions.

Because a church-sponsored social affair ought to be better than ordinary, we submit a check list to mark the progress of your preparation:

...... Publicity early and adequate?

...... Personal invitations going out?

...... Permission secured for use of premises?

...... Transportation lined up?

...... Finances under control?

...... Program well-developed and flexible?

...... Decoration and equipment adequate?

...... Food and refreshment appropriate and sufficient?

...... Insurance coverage for extended trip?

...... Definite time for beginning and ending; for departure and return home?

...... General headquarters for information?

...... Adult supervision and cooperation?

...... Does minister know and approve?

...... Is this for members only? Can they bring friends?

...... Instructions for proper clothing?

We cite these suggestions only to indicate that a social function cannot be taken for granted. The ultimate goal is to provide a sense of fellowship, of belonging to the group, and sharing in the fun.

What qualities of leadership are recommended for church recreation? The following list was composed at a recreational laboratory. The good leader:

- Has a winsome personality which makes him attractive to the group.
- Has a real and contagious love for people.
- Has a way of making people feel at home.
- Is interested in cooperative rather than competitive play.
- Is always prepared with necessary equipment.
- Always plans program well in advance.
- Deals with everyone impartially; does not play favorites.
- Does not exploit the deficiencies of persons, especially those who are awkward, homely, or peculiar.

- Does not play or permit practical jokes on anyone in the group.
- Knows when to be reverent.
- Is a good follower when someone else is leading.

(4) *Social Dancing in Church.* Should young people be permitted to dance on the church premises, or under church sponsorship, or at youth fellowship meetings? This question concerning social dancing comes up for lively debate in many situations, and therefore requires an honest appraisal.

Teenagers should have opportunities for social dancing as part of their boy-girl relationships and maturing process. Often the schools provide adequate occasions and facilities for social dancing. Some communities have public dances for teenagers, under proper supervision. Established youth centers and teen-towns, the Y.M.C.A. and Y.W.C.A., include dancing in their activities. The principal task of the Protestant church is to satisfy itself that its young people have a wholesome and satisfying outlet for dancing in the community.

If commercial dance halls and questionable places are the only available recreational centers, the church must sit up and take notice. If the beer joint and roadhouse are attractive because they have juke boxes and dance floors, the church is called to attention. If your young people flock to the youth center of a non-Protestant agency, the Protestant forces of your community must take cooperative measures.

If, therefore, your community has no normal and natural recreation centers where social dancing can be done, your church, either alone or in cooperation with other Protestant churches, must open its facilities, or secure appropriate quarters to establish a teen-town and its dairy bar, open on Friday and Saturday nights.

As for social dancing at the Sunday evening youth fellowship meeting, as part either of the group recreation or of the informal free time which may come before or after the regular meeting, our view is consistently and definitely negative. The time for a regular meeting must be concentrated on building the group spirit, the group experience, the feeling of belonging, and of being wanted.

Nothing can lower the morale of a wallflower more than to be rejected over and over again. If the youth function at church is to be another agonizing experience of rejection for shy persons, your church deliberately forces them out. While social dancing has its charms and advantages, the process of boy choosing girl divides the group into those who have, and those who haven't.

Instead of social dancing, therefore, we recommend the wealth of group dances, the folk dance, the square dance, singing and musical games. Call out, "All join hands and circle to the right," and you have what is desired—total participation.

(5) *Fellowship Singing.* Fellowship singing should also be part of the recreational life of the youth group.

A treasury of folk songs, ballads, chanties, rounds, and carols is available for pure enjoyment and camaraderie. The current popular songs and the great hymns are not usually included in this broad group of fellowship songs. Through camps and conferences, many songs are introduced and young people are quick to pick up a lively tune. The folks songs of other nations have enriched the repertoire of songs we sing in youth groups. In the general area of song-leading, we are cautioned at these points:

• Don't use action songs exclusively, though these are good starters and secure group participation.

• Don't use parodies, which twist and destroy the beauty and spirit of the original words and music.

• Don't get caught in the web of fads and favorites, but try new and other songs available in your song books.

• Don't do too much arm-waving, for such leading is sometimes confusing and objectionable.

• Know your stuff well so that you need not depend upon accompaniment or the words in the book.

• Pitch songs low enough to let the male voices share, since female voices with their wider range can sing the lower notes without strain.

• Start with songs which your group knows, and use songs which will help break down the individuality of persons.

• Know something about the background of the songs you use. A comment about each will help give it a setting.

• Use a progression of songs, deliberately planned so that your group moves from the fun and action songs, through rounds and harmonizing, to sentimental folk songs, and to more quiet and religious spirituals and hymns.

• Avoid asking for "suggestions" since the leader will then be bound by them, and no progression is possible.

• Don't ask "How many of you know this song?" By so doing the leader immediately divides the group into two. Assume they know; if they don't, teach them.

• Avoid songs which divide a group, like "This is Table No. 1." (This is the clue that the group is ready for singing.)

(6) *Dramatics.* Having fun together in the name of Christian recreation certainly includes some dramatic endeavors. With the many possibilities of using all the individuals in your youth groups, even calling on parents and children when necessary, a fling in the dramatic world is worth trying.

We are reminded at the outset that there are several avenues of dramatic expression, including some which are not stage productions, such as choral speaking, rhythmic choir, creative dramatics, plays, play-reading, pageants. For the more ambitious, there are also radio and television.

For a group of young people, whether it be a church school class or a large fellowship group of varying ages, your church could properly consider one or several dramatic experiences during the year. Easter and Christmas seem to be natural moments for dramatic plays or pageants. An evening of entertainment can be the occasion for two or three one-act plays.

One obvious advantage of dramatic activity is that it offers opportunity for creative expression, for using the many talents which your young people have, and involving probably every single one of them in a common cause. The fact that such an event calls for several weeks of combined effort suggests that it may be distinctly valuable for developing friendly cooperation and mutual assistance.

Another advantage is that through the dramatic arts some significant religious insights are taught. Participating in these arts, young people may learn to understand life from the Christian point of view and to enter into redemptive experience. Drama, then, may be much more than a "production."

Dramatic activities add variety to the church program and thus stimulate the interest of the young people. Indeed, some young person with voice, grace, or gift of expression, or with a flair for dealing with property, lighting, make-up and costuming, may find special recognition and be encouraged to develop such talent.

Drama may even call for a relatively permanent group which may pursue dramatic activity on a higher and more experienced level. Church drama, however, ought never to be limited to an exclusive circle, but ought always to be open to newcomers.

The church drama should be of high caliber, not only in its presentation and in the attitude of both actors and spectators, but in the selection of the play. Thus, for instance, a church group should not stage a minstrel show or a mock wedding. The minstrel show pokes fun at the Negro caricature, and reflects an unchristian sense of superiority over a minority group. The mock wedding makes a joke of a serious ceremony. The church seeks to make the marriage vow and the ceremony itself a religious experience. How then can a church group so casually allow the minstrel show, the mock wedding, and other low forms of entertainment?

If it's dramatics, the church has facilities, a ready-made audience, a group of willing participants, and a wide selection of suitable material. Put drama on your calendar.

COUNSELING AND GUIDANCE

In discussing the well-balanced youth program of the church, a fifth item is added to the traditional four of worship, study, service, and recreation. More and more, adult leaders become aware of the desperate need of young people "to find themselves" in this world.

How "mixed-up" the younger generation is in its ideas of right and wrong, of sexual morality, of the rights of citizenship, of war and peace, of jobs and security, and other issues of the day. The rapid movement of people, the insistent demands of advertisers, the desire for material wealth, and the ridicule of spiritual things leave the teenager with increasing uncertainty of his destiny in life.

In the high ministry of the Protestant church, it is proper then to be conscious of responsibility in giving counsel and guidance to young people. This is no new mission, of course, but worthy of more emphasis today.

There are two general avenues of approach in this matter. The first is the group approach, in which the many issues of the day, whether implicit in the church school lesson or lifted as the topic for the fellowship meeting, are openly discussed. We stress again the need for recognizing a pertinent and real question or problem, and dealing with it honestly and vigorously, with no beating around the bush.

We cherish, therefore, the permissive and free discussion, facing both sides of every issue, weighing the advantages and disadvantages of all arguments, and applying the Christian dimension to the possible solutions. Whether the individuals in the group are all participating or not, if a critical question is bravely and fairly faced in a thorough discussion, you are giving counsel and guidance. If you go hush-hush and tiptoe through some delicate question, you do a grave injustice to your adolescents, and miss the chance to help them.

The second approach is the individual face-to-face counseling. This is the more difficult, but the more effective method when properly done. Immediately one recognizes how inadequate most adult advisers and church school teachers are at this point. In many instances, the minister of the church serves as counselor for his congregation and becomes quite expert and adept at personal counseling. There are many young people, however, who hesitate to open up their concerns to their ministers.

We need only mention a few observations at this point. As a lay adult worker with young people, you can make yourself approachable for conversation by building a sense of trust and security over a period of time. This is done by your attitude and quiet observation, by being fair to all sides of a question, and mostly by letting your young people know that you do not have a "closed mind."

When a young person wants to talk over his problem, he should take the initiative. An adult counselor cannot properly go to a young person and invite a counseling situation by asking, "Let's talk about your love life." But once a face-to-face conversation is established at the request of the teenager the usual rules suggest that the adult counselor should permit the young person to talk it out, show no approval or disapproval, show no shock or horror, but indicate throughout a sense of understanding and sharing of the problem at hand. This is not the time for a lecture or a sermon. Ultimately, whatever the problem, the solution must be found by the young person himself. The task of the counselor is to suggest the possibilities open to the young person, indicate perspective and relative values, but insist that the solution rests with the young person.

It may be necessary to continue the conversation again and again. However, the counselor must never become so important in the process that unwittingly he becomes a crutch to the young person in difficulty. Of most importance is the need for absolute confidence in the conversations. If there is any indication that the situation is beyond your grasp, you should, with his permission, seek trained help immediately. This usually means the minister, and through him, such professional assistance as is necessary. We must remind ourselves over and over again that as lay adult workers, we provide only informal guidance and help. Let the professional counselor take those problems needing his attention.

Two incidents come to mind which illustrate how we have failed our young people in this respect. A girl casually mentioned that she was engaged to a Catholic fellow at college. This was after a general presentation in which we discouraged mixed marriages. Immediately, the question which ran through our mind was, where were her church, her minister, her church school teacher, and youth fellowship adviser during her growing-up teen years? With an unusually difficult home life facing her, we insist her church neglected to give her counsel and guidance.

Had she not known about the pre-nuptial agreement she would have to sign? Was she willing to raise her children in the Roman Catholic church, even perhaps to send them to a parochial school? Is she herself willing to turn Catholic, or will her religious life be a lonely experience? The most serious barrier is the denial of common family worship, of church participation, and of a common faith to carry the couple through the trying and difficult moments of married life. Surely the grace of God will guide and strengthen individuals who knowingly enter into mixed marriages. But we are convinced that some group discussions in her presence, alerting her to the hazards, and encouraging dating with Protestant boys, could have avoided this dilemma.

At another youth conference we mentioned the need for a more adequate Christian attitude toward sex. Later that day a girl asked for an interview, and she then unburdened her frightening story of being pregnant, a fact not known to her parents and church leaders. It is not inadequate sex education that we decry at this moment, but the fact that she had no understanding adult person in her home church to whom she could have gone for confidential help.

A lay adult adviser for a senior high group for five continuous years relates how his long service is now "paying off" in the many personal counseling situations into which he is called. In their dilemma facing military service, the choice of jobs or college, of relation with their parents or peers, of dating and rejection, of marriage and its implications, your young people have many hidden fears and questions. Unless your church gives answers openly or in private, with Christian implications and love, you are forcing your young people away from the church to seek answers and adjustments outside the realm of the Christian fellowship. A deliberate effort to make counseling and guidance a meaningful ministry would help to round out a balanced program for the youth of your church.

For this type of counseling, some special training is required. To read one or more books on this subject would be the first step. Some reflective thinking about actual counseling situations in which you were involved, and some situations which you missed, may give rise to more questions. If possible, you might take a short course, or discuss the many implications of counseling at meetings with other adult workers with youth. It is entirely possible that your minister may be your teacher on counseling. But finally, never consider yourself an expert or finished counselor. The implications and temptations are too profound, and you cannot lightly tamper with human lives.

This is a discipline which will be increasingly helpful as you continue to deal with people. It is for us to recognize that the church should not hesitate to deal realistically with life-shattering situations. A church group is properly called a "redemptive fellowship." Especially is this true when we recognize the strength and failures of individual lives, of the need for assurance and direction, and the confidence that each person is accepted for what he is. Thus in the redemptive fellowship, the members are concerned for each other's welfare, and in love and prayer, seek divine resources for personal problems.

Teenagers increase their confidence in the adult counselor, when the counselor:

- Shows sympathetic understanding of young people;
- Reflects forgiving love, particularly when discipline is necessary;
- Convinces the youth group that they do have the ability and the necessity to do their own critical thinking, that they can come to their own conclusions and convictions, and not be swayed by popular or peer pressure;
- Recognizes that to become a helpful counselor, he must make a tremendous effort to grow into an understanding of God's will for our lives.

CHAPTER SIX

Program Areas

WHAT MESSAGE and experience are we presenting to our young people? Why do we have the array of church school literature, expensive buildings and furnishings, trained personnel, and organizations galore? What is the unique mission of the church?

THE RELEVANCE OF THE GOSPEL

Ours is the task of presenting the Christian gospel as a declaration of truth, to and about man, from and about God. This truth demands a response. Each teenager, in his own time, will decide for or against the gospel. Thus faith is a matter of decision and commitment. In order to nurture faith and to assure intelligent, whole-hearted commitment the church school provides a thoughtfully planned, comprehensive series of lessons for each age-group. Each new course is a journey of growth in understanding. Responsible Christian educators believe that these lessons, involving a systematic study of the Christian heritage and the Christian life, are significant in the maturing spiritual lives of teenagers. Similarly, the topic material and resources for evening youth fellowship meetings are provided. These are probably more informal treatment of subjects that are to a large degree youth-centered. It is possible that young people shared in choosing topics so published.

Over the years adult persons traditionally made the decisions on the substance and direction of the youth program. The church, as conceived in adult minds, considered the following as important standards for young people: regular church attendance, personal devotions, generous gifts, concern for missions, service projects, evangelistic zeal, leadership in church functions. Youth groups list these topics as most pertinent: relations with parents, getting along with age-mates, adjustment in school life, boy-girl and dating problems, jobs and preparation for jobs. While these are self-centered concerns, the list is realistic.

The adult concerns which appear central to church leaders may deal with outward manifestations only. While attendance, giving, and the like are noble habits, the real test is the inner convictions, the compelling love, and the demanding witness. Thus grasp of the gospel and the love of God show in the maturing person, the stalwart churchman.

What then of those themes so dear to teenage souls? The problems of adjustment to themselves, to those around them, and to their future must be solved over a period of time. We are convinced that when the teenager is surrounded by Christian love and fellowship, he finds that the gospel speaks to him, even as he grapples with his personal problems. The outward practice of zeal, devotion, and service may also contribute to a healthy understanding of selfhood.

A common complaint is that the church school lesson or the topic material is not pertinent to young people. This may be true if the focus is on either extreme, the outward manifestations or the personal problems. Seen in the light of the gospel which is relevant to the growing adolescent and the world in which he lives, each lesson and topic can contribute to the spiritual maturing of the individual.

The ultimate Christian education task is to confront each person with the Christian gospel, which he may accept or reject. The hope, of course, is that he will accept and commit his life to God through Christ. A "first commitment" can reasonably be expected during his early teenage years. However, constant and frequent experiences to help him grow in his understanding are necessary. Thus rededication, recommitment, and renewed consecration are valid and desirable phases of growth. To provide these experiences is the unique task of your church.

THE COMMISSION PLAN

To cope with the many aspects of churchmanship and to deal fairly with the problems of teenage growth, the local church needs to organize its resources and material. The grouping of the areas of church concern in simple units would help in planning the youth program. There should also be distinct guideposts to assure a broad base of study and experience.

Representative youth leaders have studied the many segments of youth concern, and agreed on five major divisions. Each division is a grouping of church-related subjects, and within it is a related core. The "Plan for Common Commissions in Christian Youth Work" was evolved in the United Christian Youth Movement, and became generally acceptable to the various denominations. The plan recognizes the basic items of program and study which young people need in the process of maturing toward adult churchmanship. It divides these program items into five groupings called commissions, or program areas. Within each commission are listed several "areas of concern."

The advantages of such a plan are obvious. If Christian faith, for instance, is an emphasis in one denomination, the young people of another denomination can easily share its activities. As new literature, projects, audio-visuals, and other instructive material are prepared, the commission plan can easily channel the responsibilities. When the annual interdenominational Youth Week emphasis bears on one of the five commissions, this makes sense to those denominations which operate on the plan. For churches of several denominations in a given community, the plan makes it possible to bring their young people together and talk a common language.

Under this plan it is possible for helpful projects, audio-visuals, or pieces of literature in one denomination to be borrowed and adapted in another. The production of a series of filmstrips on youth work could scarcely have been done by one denomination alone. But because of the commission plan, twelve denominations were able to pool funds and personnel to produce the Youth Audio-Visual Series of seven sound filmstrips.

Probably of greater importance is the impact on young people in the local church. The division of the many program items into five groupings makes it possible to maintain a balance of emphasis, a greater dimension of interest, a wider scope of activity, and better training for adult churchmanship.

Some churches have grouped the divisions into three commission areas, while retaining all the substance of the five. The five groupings, together with the adaptations when these are combined into three, are:

COMMISSIONS OR PROGRAM AREAS

1. Christian Faith   }
2. Christian Witness   } 1. Christian Faith

3. Christian Outreach   }
4. Christian Citizenship   } 2. Christian Action

5. Christian Fellowship   3. Christian Fellowship

These words now become infused with great implications. Practically everything that is valid in the Protestant church and its youth program has a natural place under the headings indicated. Consider the scope and intent of the five program areas. The purposes are phrased as suggested by the United Christian Youth Movement.

CHRISTIAN FAITH

The purpose of presenting Christian faith to our young people is "to help youth grow in a vital Christian faith and life." All the activities, topics, experiences, and emphases which strengthen the inner convictions, the Christian commitment, and spiritual strength of each of your young people are comprehended in this area of concern.

(1) *Christian Beliefs.* The study of Christian beliefs can be done over a series of meetings, by the careful reading of an appropriate book, with discussion topics, by the use of films and filmstrips, and by an occasional speaker. One must recall that the teenager's grasp of his faith, and beliefs fluctuates, and that he needs constant assurance and reassurance. Every opportunity for engaging in honest discussion, for expressing questions and doubts, for strengthening one's beliefs should be provided. Here is the place for insisting on sound theology, for intellectual consistency with what the young people learn in school, and integrity in your denominational heritage.

Your young people may already have studied some of the significant subjects which relate to one's beliefs: Jesus, God, the Bible, man, the church, the kingdom, death, salvation, suffering, prayer, and the sacraments. But you can properly insist that one exposure is inadequate, that an annual review is helpful, and sometimes most needed. Growing minds also suggest growing spirits.

(2) *Personal Christian Commitment.* The final goal of youth work is sincere Christian commitment of each young person. We are convinced that the valid commitment of a person comes only after a series of significant experiences including some basic studies, some wrestling within one's self, with facing of problems of the day, and in company with other seekers of the Christian way.

While real commitment can never be directly measured, it

is outwardly revealed by the spirit of service, humility, steward-ship, and devotion. It is the church's task to seek continually for Christian commitment, for the deepening and strengthening of one's conviction, and for the cultivation of the Christian fellowship.

Obviously, talking about commitment will not suffice. The lives of adult teachers, parents, and leaders become the shining examples by which the truth of commitment becomes known. Stories of committed persons in the Bible, in history, and in current life may also point up the goal we seek.

(3) *Personal Enrichment and Growth.* Bible study, personal devotions, prayer, worship, and cell group experiences contrib-ute to personal enrichment and growth. In the church school and the youth fellowship meeting, many aspects of the daily strengthening of the inner spirit are studied. Group excursions into such questions as "What is prayer?" "Who wrote the Bible?" and "How do we worship?" are to be encouraged. A spiritual life retreat may be a major project in this area.

(4) *Personal Conduct.* In this day of moral confusion, our young people need spiritual guideposts which are pertinent and appropriate to their lives. Cheating in school, sexual license, breaking laws and rules, vandalism, malicious gossip, and other temptations of the day need to be faced and aired. Certainly there are basic Christian truths which speak for personal integ-rity, concern for the welfare of others, and responsibility to the community.

(5) *The Christian Heritage.* Protestant young people must be reminded of the heritage which comes to us from the Refor-mation. The history of your denomination needs to be made clear to each member of your teenage group. With the easy mobility of our generation, denominational differences seem to fade. Yet one chooses to belong to a denominational family, and in the choosing, one needs to glory in its traditions.

(6) *Meaning of Church Membership.* While denominations and churches differ in their practice of receiving teenagers into responsible church membership, it is true that young people are usually received into membership during early adolescence. This follows a series of lessons in a long-term confirmation or catechetical class, or in a brief series of "church membership" sessions. It is important that the young people realize the meaning and significance of church membership, and the privileges and responsibilities which are theirs.

CHRISTIAN WITNESS

The purpose of this commission or program area is "to help youth make known to others the way of Christ by all they say and do." A Christian young person, once his inner convictions become stabilized, needs to express his commitment in Christian witness.

(1) *Evangelism.* Is the experience of asking another person to come to church, to join the church school class or youth fellowship group, and to become a Christian an ordeal? It may become a source of unexpected strength. To call on another in behalf of the church may appear odd enough, but the spirit of inviting others needs to become a natural part of the program of Christian youth. This evangelistic outreach of your church can be done on a dignified plane. On a youth-to-youth basis, carried out by individuals or as a planned group activity, evangelism ought to be an important phase of your church's work. An annual visitation program at the beginning of a school year might well become a tradition at your church.

(2) *Stewardship.* The sense of stewardship is easily grasped by young people. In facing the demands of the Christian gospel, they need to place their contribution of time and talent in proper perspective. Stewardship is not to be measured in hours or dollars, but in spirit and faithfulness.

Hence, in projects of service, of giving money, of lending aid, and in other manifestations of Christian life young people need to evaluate their acts and check their motives. What did it mean to raise money for the building fund, and by what means was the money raised? Did singing carols for the shut-ins do justice to our self-esteem, or were we honestly serving our fellowmen?

(3) *Churchmanship.* Church membership must be more than token listing on the church roll, the privilege of taking Communion, and sharing in the church budget. The significance of membership needs to be lifted in many ways. This can be accomplished by encouraging young people to share in the Sunday church service, help perhaps in the liturgy, in ushering, in singing in the choir, and similar exercises on a Sunday morning. As individuals they can take their part in congregational activities such as visitation evangelism, community surveys, the every-member canvass, pledging toward a building fund, serving on established and temporary committees of the church.

(4) *Christian Vocation.* Traditionally, we look upon the professional minister, missionary, and director of Christian education as ultimate expressions of Christian life. More and more we are shifting our view and saying that every person, man or woman, educated or not, can be truly a Christian person in whatever work or task he has at hand. This emphasis seeks a dedication of our talents to God in our daily lives. Thus we give our lives meaning and value.

In so saying, we recognize that your church may not be equipped to give adequate vocational counseling. It is, however, your duty to instill in youthful minds the fact that their choice of jobs must be made in light of the Christian concept of service. A public school teacher, a journalist, a public official, as well as the homemaker and the tradesman, all have a share in the building of the kingdom through their daily tasks.

Wholly apart from money-earning jobs, mature Christians find opportunities of service in community agencies, church and public welfare channels, and youth-serving organizations on a voluntary basis. This, too, is Christian vocation.

CHRISTIAN OUTREACH

The purpose of this commission is "to help youth know, and accept their responsibility in, the world-wide mission of the church."

(1) *Home Missions.* The purpose of this major arm of our church effort has been to "evangelize America." Keeping up with a rapidly moving population is both an expensive and a challenging story in the life of the denominations. Since the second world war the population has been moving from rural to industrial centers, from downtown to suburban communities, from East and Midwest to Pacific Coast and Gulf states. Our denominational boards have planted churches right and left to minister to new communities which sprout overnight.

The shifting population also leaves its mark in the downtown sections of our big cities, where tensions between races and social classes make life miserable for thousands. Too often the established downtown church has moved to the so-called better sections of town. Yet the lives of those in these deteriorating neighborhoods need the impact of the Christian gospel, and the church serves through community and neighborhood centers in their midst.

The rural scene is also changing. Small churches, unable to hold full-time ministers and with decreasing memberships, need to review the situation. Through the Town and Country departments of our home mission boards, the churches are at work.

While the United States may properly be called a "melting pot," there are "islands" of minority people to whom the churches reach out in Christian compassion. These are Amer-

ican Indians, Orientals, Spanish-speaking Americans, and Negroes. Home mission work also extends to Alaska, Hawaii, and
the Caribbean.

For our young people, the exciting story of this missionary
effort to keep alive the Christian gospel among our own people,
within our national borders, can be lifted with study, with films,
with visits, and with interviews. There may be a mission center
or project nearby to which your young people can be helpfully
related. Consult the director of the project and explore the
possibilities. The spirit and life of your church, indeed the
"mission of the church" is here tested.

(2) *Foreign Missions.* Rapid communication and transportation have changed some terminology we long have associated
with the missionary enterprise abroad. This was once "foreign"
missions. Now "foreign" missions is also called "international"
missions and "overseas" missions. Success was measured in
converts among the natives, who are now called nationals.
Where there was glory in the number of denominational ban-
ners flying abroad, now there are "indigenous" churches, and
"young" churches.

With increasing sensitivity to intrusion, and a rise of national-
ism and pride in their own heritage, the people abroad to whom
missionaries were sent appear to block our efforts. While some
areas of the world have been closed or become more restrictive,
the need for bringing the Christian gospel to all people is
still present.

There are several approaches to missionary work abroad.
Church representatives are engaged in educational, medical,
agricultural, as well as the usual evangelistic ministry. This calls
for more trained personnel with specialized education. Probably
the biggest witness is not what is conveyed through the teaching
and healing ministry, but in the relationships and attitudes our
people maintain to those whom we serve.

There is no denying that the task is difficult. Yet the lives of millions of people are shrouded in the darkness of illiteracy, disease, superstition, malnutrition, and ignorance. They have been subjugated for years under tyranny and fear, and their daily struggle for food and shelter make America's comfortable lives incongruous.

To bring the needs of the world close to the consciences and the hearts of your young people, you are pressed to awaken in them a sense of responsibility as members of the Christian family. Your denomination, through your missionary board, makes available information on missionary activities in which your churches are engaged. You should also know of the helpful and instructive books, films, maps, plays, and other material produced every year with the imprint of Friendship Press. Cooperating in the Commission on Missionary Education (CME), your denomination shares in developing common themes for each year, one on home missions, and another on foreign missions, providing reading and study material for the various age-groups.

There are separate series for junior highs and for senior highs, and most study books come with leader's guides. Most of the fellowship topics include the use of these books and films. Since the over-all theme is used in common across the country, there are many opportunities within a given congregation to hold a mission institute, to present a film or play, or even a special speaker on the general theme, and divide into age-groups to pursue the topic appropriate to each level. The JCME themes also suggest interdenominational and community activities, rallies and conferences.

Your concern for missionary activities often includes the raising of money for designated projects. This practice may differ from church to church, but it is true that the giving of money, preferably through the established channels of the congregation, becomes an expression of youth concern. Be alert to your denomination's program of supporting the church budget, both of the local congregation and the denomination. Again, far more important than the money, or the amount of the money, is the study of the need of your church to be active in bringing the Christian gospel to all people.

We offer a word of caution on the attitude which young people usually take toward others. Americans are apt to look with a superior air on those we serve. Our high standard of living, educational and technical achievements, military and political influences, and other earmarks of the blessings of the abundant life gives us a "chosen people" complex. We become impatient with those who differ from us in philosophy, language, and custom. By all means, this should be brought to light and properly evaluated.

There are many persons from abroad studying or working in America. Your missionary study can be enriched by having the participation of one or several of these persons in your program.

(3) *The Ecumenical Movement.* Most of our denominations are related to the National Council of Churches of Christ in the United States of America. This gives us a channel for expressing our common faith and duty, and offers guidance and direction to each of the participating denominations in various segments of church life.

Beyond the United States, our churches are related to the World Council of Churches, and the World Council of Christian Education and Sunday School Association. Through these agencies we join hands in a combined witness of Protestant and Orthodox churches around the world. The two agencies have youth departments which work together. In the world scene, they express the concern of churches for youth from 18 to 30, develop united ecumenical action, help to provide effective Christian education, and develop a sense of unity and fellowship. Leadership training courses are held, youth leaders are exchanged, overseas visits arranged, a newssheet is published in several languages, ecumenical work-camps are sponsored, international meetings are held, youth work materials are assembled, and World Youth Projects are cleared. In addition, both agencies have executive personnel who counsel with youth leaders around the world.

Give special attention to recent world conferences, especially when young people of your denomination are sent as delegates. The Union of Latin American Evangelical Youth (ULAJE) needs the support and encouragement of young people in the United States. Through our United Christian Youth Movement, we are all intimately related to these activities.

Of real pertinence is your participation in the World Youth Projects, through which youth groups give financial and moral aid to youth programs in the four corners of the world. Do names like Burma, Honduras, Madagascar, Nigeria, Germany, Spain, South Africa, Korea, Brazil, and even American Indians stimulate your imagination? Your youth group is sharing in strengthening the youth work in these and many other areas of the world. Be alert to them, and learn something of this work.

(4) *Inter-church Aid.* While the immediate ravages of the second world war may have diminished, the Protestant churches are still conscious of human needs in places of tension and emergency across the world. Relief clothing is still needed, orphan children still require shelter. Heifers, plows, chicks, and seeds dramatize the kind of gifts which rebuild self-reliance and independence. Money and personnel stand ready to serve where emergency strikes, and Church World Service represents most of us in this endeavor.

The small but significant beginnings in the ecumenical work-camp program, bringing together several hundred young persons from many national backgrounds to serve destitute situations, reflect again an outreach of youth concern. This story can be told and retold, in film or in person. There is also the happy exchange of teenage students, bringing young people of other nations into our communities and sending our high school students to spend some months and years abroad. Inquire about the possibilities of participating in the International Christian Youth Exchange, a church-sponsored high-school level program.

(5) *Peace and World Order.* While our generation of young people has known war and threats of war, it is for the church to dream and build in terms of peace and world order. The United Nations and its organizations need the support of your church people. Though United Nations Day is in late October, frequent attention might be called to its work. A continuous concern for peace is an unavoidable Christian duty. Your young people should wrestle with the problems raised by the military fever of the nation.

CHRISTIAN CITIZENSHIP

This commission is "to help youth understand community needs and, on the basis of Christian convictions, work to meet these needs through personal influence and group action."

(1) *Service to the Local Church and Community.* Active participation in the life of the local church and community should be flavored with the sense of personal responsibility. Especially is this true for teenagers. Their contributions can be made in group projects involving physical activities. From the care and maintenance of the physical properties of the church building to the mending and repairing of hymnbooks and furnishings, your young people can find meaningful outlet and satisfying achievement.

Similarly, the immediate community may use the combined manpower of your group to tackle a problem or job, suitable for adolescent bodies and minds. A probable approach on any project will call for three steps. First is the gathering of data and facts to see the whole scope of the problem. Second, the group should do some critical discussion, weighing the implications of Christian concern and duty. Then, third, some appropriate work project may result.

(2) *Inter-group Relations.* In preparation for their own adult citizenship, Christian youth must face the difficult problems which arise from competing and differing forces within our national life. We are conscious of the tremendous adjustments necessary to ease the interracial situation. Most sensitive in this respect are Protestant church leaders who are aware that church people have not been the positive witnesses on this subject. The Negro-white solution will call for Christian compassion and love. Youth groups are not yet burdened with the cares of "property values" and sentimental attachments to forge ahead into interracial experiences.

Our people take an offensive attitude toward those of the Jewish faith, and bemoan the loss of our young people to the Roman Catholic church in mixed marriages. An open and fair study in this interfaith area during impressionable teenage years is an important contribution of your ministry.

In your community may live a group of people representing other cultural backgrounds, whether recent immigrants or the remnants of a foreign-language settlement. It is to your advantage to seek first-hand contact to enrich the understanding of your young people.

(3) *Industrial Relations and Economic Issues.* Are your church people conscious of the capital-labor strife? What is the feeling of your young people when a strike is called in a major industry in your town? What is the role of your church in interpreting this tension in the light of the Christian gospel? Your teenagers will reflect home and parental sentiments on this

subject, but a fair hearing of "the other side" is certainly in order. In dealing with these relationships, church school lessons, meeting topics, venturesome projects, and visits, tours, and special study are all sources of insight and Christian understanding.

(4) *Social Problems*. Christian citizenship gets tested again in its attitude and activities in dealing with the problems of alcohol, dope addiction, gambling, juvenile delinquency, and other social ills. Too often, we merely deplore and pass resolutions to outlaw this, that, and the other. We must recognize that there are many contributory factors, and therefore many solutions. What then can you in your church do to prepare your teenagers to face these destructive influences? What are some helpful ways in which the contributing factors may be relieved?

On a wider scale, if Christian citizenship is to have deeper significance, your young people might want to witness the workings of the town or city hall, the community court house, the state capital, and even perhaps the national capital. Within reason, this can be a significant experience. And there are Christian politicians who might tell your group how future citizens can participate more actively in governmental affairs.

CHRISTIAN FELLOWSHIP

The purpose of this commission is "to help youth experience in all their relationships the bond of Christian fellowship which comes from their common faith." This commission is interested in the Christian-to-other-Christians relationships.

(1) *The Local Church*. Every effort should be made to integrate the young people into the life and activities of the local church. After all is said and done, the young people belong to this church, and membership and relationship there should be normal and pleasant. Therefore, their hopes and

wishes should be given a fair hearing. One usual obstacle is the denial of adequate recreational facilities and leadership. Another is ignoring young people by not providing leadership, classes, or program.

The young people should cooperate to the best of their ability in all phases of the congregational program. Membership in committees and boards, participation in drives, campaigns, and emphases, and sponsorship of all-church activities are within the youth realm. These all-church functions may include picnic, fun-night, banquet, talent show, work project, and the like.

(2) *Christian Home Life.* The church should help parents understand teenagers, and at the same time urge young people to make the necessary adjustments to make home livable. Grievances and misunderstandings between parents and youth can be ironed out in group functions at church. Occasions which bring them together are desirable.

(3) *Boy-Girl Relations.* Boy-girl friendships undoubtedly motivate the attendance of many young people at church functions. This is not only a happy coincidence, but an opportunity to help them understand themselves, and each other. The whole realm of friendship, dating, courtship, and marriage needs thorough study and discussion. The matter of Christian attitudes on sex should be stressed. For those girls and boys who seem friendless and dateless, some positive program should be launched to involve them, and to encourage their social life.

(4) *Recreation.* While good times, food, and fun may characterize our youth program, Christian fellowship demands that recreation have high standards. Through the activities of the church, young people learn social graces, meet new people, and become adept at leadership themselves.

(5) *Inter-church Relations.* Your young people must have definite relationship with the youth fellowship of your denom-

ination. This may mean attendance at an occasional conference or rally, or can mean some form of "joining" with the national group. At least once each year, your young people should also participate in some interdenominational activity or function. This can easily be a Youth Week experience (last Sunday in January to first Sunday in February). Your young people should be related, consciously and deliberately, to the local, state, and national levels of the United Christian Youth Movement. Two or more churches in your community may form a Christian youth council to work on a common project.

(6) *Leisure Time.* Leisure time of your young people can be either constructive or destructive, depending upon the encouragement your church provides in facilities, ideas, and leadership. It is within the responsibilities of Christian fellowship to be concerned in this area, and to seek suggestions and help. An occasional hobby show will be revealing.

(7) *Creative Arts.* Creative arts is the term to cover all those activities one associates with drama, music, crafts, and related fields. These are vehicles which lead your young people to Christian growth by working together, gaining proficiency in the field, and providing wholesome entertainment for others. A major project in this field can be an annual affair.

(8) *The Armed Forces and Conscientious Objectors.* For those members of the group who have gone from the local scene to military service or who have become conscientious objectors, there should be some regular and systematic program of keeping in touch. Writing letters, sending bulletins, and remembering birthdays are common. To welcome them on their visits home is important. Set up the machinery so that those who leave will still feel some roots in the home church.

THE PLAN AT WORK

For the effective working of the commission plan the first need is to recognize the content and substance of the plan, listed and described in these pages. The second is to provide structure and organization under which the content may best be presented. What are some possible organizational patterns?

One approach is to appoint a chairman for each of the five (or three) program areas of the commission plan. It will be the responsibility of the chairman to seek for the best presentation of the particular concerns of his commission, to insist on a fair share of attention to his program areas, and to maintain a group consciousness of the purpose of his commission.

For instance, the chairman responsible for Christian witness will become an "expert" on the subjects of evangelism, stewardship, churchmanship, and Christian vocation. At least he will know what these words mean. He will also know what books, lesson material, topic resources, films and filmstrips, local persons, and committees are available to him. He will be responsible for seeing that a full treatment of any or each of his areas is presented to his church school class or evening fellowship meeting. He will promote a major project, perhaps of youth evangelism, or the every-member canvass. He may be the youth member on the congregation's finance committee or evangelism committee. He will have the names and addresses of the Christian witness chairman of his region, district, state, synod, convention, or conference, and the National Council of his denominational Youth Fellowship. He will seek opportunities to attend training conferences and institutes. He will be alert to articles, releases, books, and magazines dealing on his subjects.

All this and more are the privileges and expectations of the youth chairman of a program area. Each of the other commission chairmen will carry a similar task. These chairmen sit on the youth council or cabinet as executive officers to correlate planning and activities.

A second approach is to appoint three, four, or five persons to each commission. All the tasks mentioned above now become the responsibility of a group of persons. This is particularly helpful if, for instance, the Commission on Christian Outreach is responsible for the program of an evening fellowship meeting. The members of this commission will make plans for the whole evening, including the worship, topic presentation and discussion, and the recreation period. Such a unified program should be the pattern of any evening presentation by a commission group.

A third approach is to assign every member of the whole youth fellowship to each of the five (or three) commissions. Each commission then is a working group, and in addition to all the tasks listed above, it may engage in other activities as a separate small-group. Thus, an individual who joins the church's youth groups, is invited to one of the commission small-groups. If his commission is responsible for Christian fellowship, he finds the members specializing not only in recreation, but in drama, boy-girl, home life, and other Christian fellowship responsibilities. He may himself concentrate on creative arts, especially choral speech. This may become his contribution to the commission group, and to the total group.

A fourth approach is not to name any chairman, or to appoint commission members, or to divide the total group into the five (or three) program area groups. The total group concentrates, by common consent, on one of the program areas for a given period, say, two or three months. This is particularly suitable for the junior high age-group, whose intellectual background is inadequate to take on the kind of tasks required for individual or small-group leadership.

As for the rotation of membership and responsibilities under the first three approaches, a half-year to one year is advisable. Any one area has enough material and potential for a young person to grow in Christian faith and life. It is better for young people to become proficient in a few things than to cover the waterfront superficially.

The commission plan is not a cure-all for programming or for organization. This plan provides a guide and a balance, to assure adequate treatment of the many concerns of good church-manship. Local adaptation and variations are always possible. Look to denominational suggestions for seasonal and united emphases.

CHAPTER SEVEN

Clues for Better Meetings

WHAT ARE SOME basic elements of a good youth meeting? How can we secure good attendance, participation, and sustained interest? What ought we to expect from the regular Sunday night meetings?

A YOUTH FELLOWSHIP MEETING

The regular week-by-week meeting of the evening youth fellowship group requires planning, preparation, presentation, and follow-up. Each meeting should be balanced with worship, study, and fun. These elements can be expressed in a central theme. Of course, a youth fellowship meeting can be a haphazard affair, with little preparation, crudely composed, and indifferently presented. Because one of these meetings may be the first or only exposure to church experience for many young people, it is important that considerable time and attention be given to the meeting plans.

While local tradition and situations dictate what usually goes on, we describe here a desirable, typical youth fellowship meeting.

(1) *Planning.* For each meeting, a committee of three, four, or five persons should outline and plan the structure, sequence, emphasis, and substance of the evening. The committee may be an established group, carrying this responsibility for several meetings, or may be appointed for this one occasion. With the

help of an adult, the evening's program should be reviewed and double-checked, so that last-minute absences will not cause embarrassing omissions.

(2) *Publicity.* Some ingenious system of constant publicity for youth fellowship meetings will assure a high level of attendance. This can include post-card reminders, phone calls, posters, handouts, invitations, and other methods of creating suspense and interest. A notice in the church bulletin is not enough. Button-holing at church in the morning will help. Special effort to contact and invite those who attend occasionally is also desirable.

(3) *Pre-meeting.* Make special provision for pre-meeting activities, such as informal recreation, a browsing table, a conversation corner.

(4) *Worship.* Whether the devotional period comes at the beginning, during, or at the end of the evening program may be determined for each meeting. Nevertheless, careful and adequate preparation for this period should help each individual experience a vital and significant moment of the presence of God.

(5) *Topic.* Each youth fellowship meeting should center around the topic of the evening. While the selection of the topic may have been made through long-range planning, the actual preparation and presentation must now be made with careful precision. There are four phases to this part of the meeting.

(a) *Presentation of Topic.* Every topic must be put before the group in some manner or another. This can be done by a speech, a guest speaker, a film, filmstrip, or record, by a picture, skit, reading, debate, panel, or role-play. The subject matter can be drawn from a group visit, a research project, an interview, a trip by a member, an accident or incident, a death or birth, or some community situation. The theme of the evening can also be determined by the holiday or season of the year.

The day's topic must be carefully placed before the people. Imagination, ingenuity, and initiative can be combined to make each meeting a fresh experience. An effective presentation at this point lifts the three other phases to meaningful levels. While many persons prefer to make their speeches without the aid of props or equipment, there are those who make elaborate use of the chalkboard, turn-over sheets, prepared charts, and other visual aids. It is also possible to have a voice come over the public address system, or by way of a tape-recorder.

Depending upon the nature of the topic, this presentation may be short or long. Ultimately, something must be before the group to look at and digest.

(b) *General Discussion*. Once the subject matter has been presented, the young people should have opportunity to ask questions, clear misunderstandings, challenge the facts or figures, comment favorably or unfavorably upon the statements made, and contribute other observations not yet mentioned. They should be encouraged to enter into the discussion in the spirit of give and take, recognize the different points of view, identify the sources of tension, suggest possible solutions, and get a fair grasp of the major presentation. This discussion period is aimed especially to help each person understand the substance of the subject matter.

(c) *The "So What" Discussion*. No topic presented to a youth fellowship group should be left stranded in mid-air. In everything said and done, each person should ask himself, "So what does this say to me, a Christian?" In truth, every person should undergo some difficult soul-searching and personal scrutiny at this moment. If the discussion was on some area of race relations, it is not enough that an interesting and novel film on brotherhood was seen, and a stimulating discussion followed. Well, what does this say to the young people?

In the original planning for the meeting, the key question at this point should be anticipated. Is there any shortcoming in our individual lives? If the topic was on some area of steward-ship, and the church treasurer presented the church budget for information and evaluation, what does this say to that young person who only recently became a responsible communicant member of the church? Yes, so what?

It is recognized that it is ticklish and sensitive business for the Christian gospel to "meddle" in private affairs. Yet this is precisely the time and place for the young person to evaluate his conscience, his motive, his level of life. Does he respond in a Christian manner? Is he sensitive to human needs? Has he faithfully observed his responsibility in light of his Christian commitment?

The danger, of course, is to pass lightly over these questions. Church people are so willing to be comfortable and proper, to permit the professional minister and others to live the good life. It is an insult to youth to tolerate easy answers, the casual attitude, the superficial reaction. Young people are able to deal honestly and vigorously with the issues of the day.

Indeed, if a new and varied presentation is essential in the first phase of topic presentation, the demanding and insistent review of Christian commitment is even more important. For some young person, this may be the first time that a Christian challenge is placed before him. It is truly a sacred moment in the evening's program, and adequate time for this phase must be anticipated.

(d) *Action!* The fourth and final phase comes in pulling together everything that has been said so far, the general understanding of the topic, and its implications for individual lives. Determine whether the facts of the day impose upon this group some necessary next steps. What does the group do now, in the light of the conclusions? Is it safe to go away and let the problem take care of itself? Depending upon the topic, there should be some specific and aggressive response. The least of such responses is a short and spontaneous moment of consecration, of confession, of commitment. This may be the time for a public expression by one or another person of a hope or dream.

The other possibility is the adoption of a daring and challenging program or project to cope with the issues presented in the topic. For instance, the topic may have dealt with boy-girl relationships, for which the presentation and discussion were quite illuminating. Until the Christian interpretation and discipline were applied, the individuals discussed the subject in an off-handed and disinterested manner. But now there may be the realization that many persons in the group have been conducting themselves in unwholesome and dangerous ways. In their distress, they ask for guidance and strength. Many possible solutions may be suggested: the church to sponsor Friday night teen-town; the adviser to secure personal counselors for private consultations; the proposal of a six-week study on dating and courtship; a period of guided prayer and private meditation. Any one or all of these can be the outcome of this meeting.

It follows, then, that no youth fellowship meeting can be honestly dismissed until the topic presentation is brought to this proper conclusion. What this means in the life of the young person, and in the course of the youth group is both terrifying and wonderful. For here, at last, is the group and the time when life-molding situations are confronted by Christian interpretations.

While most topics can be drawn to a close in all four phases within the allotted time of an evening's program, sometimes the young persons may be so concerned and anxious that subsequent meeting time is needed to satisfy the members. This, of course, should be allowed. The other alternative is to cut into the recreation time, or even to eliminate the period of recreation for that evening.

(6) *Recreation Period*. As a general rule every evening's program should have some moments for relaxed group rec-

reation. This may be fellowship singing, some quiet parlor games, some paper and pencil activities, and other possibilities. Whether refreshment is served or not, and how frequently if at all, is a matter for local choice.

(7) *The Business Meeting.* There are always some necessary announcements to be made, details to be ironed out, and future plans reviewed. If the youth group looks upon itself as an organization or a club, it is perfectly reasonable to expect it to act in parliamentary procedure, keep profuse records, maintain a treasury, be encumbered by a host of standing and temporary committees, thrash out innumerable details of old and new business, and have a merry time in the process. Such a group will call the roll, collect dues, hear the minutes of the previous meeting, receive financial reports, get committee reports, and move on to old business and new business. It is entirely conceivable that a youth group can spend the whole evening in this routine, and do so from meeting to meeting through the year.

On the other hand, if the youth group of a Protestant church looks upon its evening fellowship meeting as an opportunity for Christian application to the issues of life, to challenge and stimulate the minds and hearts of young people in worship, study, and play, and to cement the bonds of fellowship, the whole tone and nature of the evening's program is different. There is then no need for, and indeed, no time for a business meeting.

Is the roll call necessary? Attendance is important, but probably the only required count is the total attendance at each meeting. Names of visitors and newcomers may be registered. Are minutes of the meeting to be kept? While detailed and accurate records have their place, the youth fellowship group is not established for long and honored existence. On the contrary, the secretary can make herself responsible for being the historian of the group, to note the outstanding events of each meeting, the activities and general evaluation of other functions, and other significant data. A scrapbook of programs, invitations, photographs, clippings, and correspondence may be assigned to the secretary. She can also keep the bulletin board up to date.

What about dues? If we are agreed that this is a fellowship group open to all comers, then dues are immediately discarded. To count membership on a basis of paid-up status is to look upon this group as a club, an organization. Of course money is essential to keep the program moving. We favor the elimination of the treasury and bank account in the name of the youth group. Have access, however, to the funds of the church for budget items.

Probably the business meeting made its best contribution in securing program ideas, establishing decisions of major or minor importance, and arousing general support for the program and functions of the group. We would rather see the program planning session take place at a special time for this purpose, and details for agreed functions settled by the executive cabinet, a specially appointed committee, or an established commission or small-group. All that is required then is time for general announcements, approval of basic decisions, and opportunity to clear final arrangements. Young people should become sensitive to the group process, the need for adequate discussion, the stimulation of group responsibility, and the molding of the group mind. Thus, whether in a small executive meeting, or if necessary in the large total group, decisions should be reached "by common consent."

(8) *Adjournment*. A definite adjournment time is highly recommended. Teenage young people can be assumed to have school assignments; some persons have transportation to take into account; parents reasonably expect their children home at a given time. While older teenagers may indulge in after-meeting activities away from the church, the official church responsibility should terminate at a clearly defined moment.

Bring the meeting to a close in a fitting and dignified manner. Your church may have found a pattern which has become traditional and significant. Others may find that their young people slip out in twos and threes and that the meeting disintegrates without a formal closing. You might close with the friendship circle, with a moment of quiet reflection, the singing of one stanza of a hymn, a prayer or two, and the group benediction. A friendy good night will send them on their way. Make certain, however, that the planning committee has arranged for the necessary clean-up, rearranging furniture, cleaning up the kitchen, and closing the building.

For the desirable typical meeting, we might think of the following time schedule:

6:30	Pre-meeting activities
7:00	Worship
7:20	Topic
8:00	Recreation
8:30	Adjournment

There can be any number of variations and adjustments in this basic schedule. The sequence of worship-topic-recreation can be shifted occasionally. The time for topic can be extended or shortened, as can the time for recreation. A group may devote one whole meeting to planning for subsequent meetings and activity assignments, by the total group or by smaller groups. There are some young people who give all of one meeting to an evening of recreation. Some groups hold a one-hour meeting, and some may hold two-hour meetings. There are also groups which precede or terminate the meeting with a supper, either every time or occasionally.

All of these possibilities are before the local church. Recognizing that communities and churches differ in size and location, it is not fair to insist that one pattern is the only way. We feel, however, that many of the principles and reasons we have stressed are valid whether the youth group has five active members, or fifty, or 150. The final judgment which measures the effective youth program is based on the impact of the program on the individual and on the group. We work and pray to make sure that this is a Christian impact.

(9) *Evaluation.* The members of the committee in charge should find time to agree on the success or failure of the several elements of the meeting. Their notes may be available for reference, to improve succeeding meetings.

STARTING A NEW GROUP

Young people come in waves in the life of the local church. Sometimes there may be a preponderance of boys, or of girls. For two or three years there may be only a few teenage people; then there may be a large group of fifteen to twenty coming into the junior high division.

Occasionally, the group is well-knit, and has a number of aggressive, active leaders. Again there may be a number of persons but no apparent leaders. When the church is without a pastor, the youth program has been known to die. A new minister may take a church and find that nothing has been done in the youth program for many years. Similarly, the presence or absence of an effective adult leader may create the cycle of a good or a poor year for youth activities.

Assuming that attention is given to the Sunday morning church school class for teenage people, you may wish to provide some organization or program for the young people themselves. These are the possible steps.

(1) *Let the minister or an adult person sit down with two or three young people and talk about the possibility of organizing an evening youth fellowship group.* Mention the kind of activities that are in store for such a group: meeting informally in some person's home, enjoying social functions, having opportunity to talk about topics of interest to themselves, attending

a youth rally of their denomination, serving the church in some useful way.

(2) *When they are satisfied that an evening fellowship group is possible, they proceed to list all the names of those who may be called together.* The church school roster, their friends at school, the minister's contacts, and other sources provide a ready list. Perhaps there is already a natural group: the church school class, a basketball team, a youth choir, or a scout troop.

(3) *A steering committee of young people may plan two or three informal social functions to bring them together.* These can be a picnic, a swim, an outing, a hayride, a fun-night at church, meeting in someone's basement. The idea is to get the persons to feel at home with one another.

(4) *Maybe a specific task can be done:* putting on an Easter program; serving a supper; some work project at the church. Without fuss or bother, have these young people meet to do something together. This, too, prepares them to feel part of a group.

(5) *At one of these occasions, a young person may suggest a discussion meeting.* Depending upon the local situation, the topics can be suggested by the original steering committee. Appoint another committee to arrange for this "first meeting." Make renewed efforts to reach every possible young person with a personal invitation. Plan a simple but adequate program.

(6) *This first meeting can start with a period of ice-breakers, fellowship singing, and a short devotional period.* A filmstrip on some missionary activity of the church may open the group to a general discussion. Let the adult leader or minister summarize. Play a few parlor games, have light refreshment, sing a few more songs, and end with a friendship circle. Before dismissing the group, ask casually whether the group would like to meet again. If so, then appoint another small committee to plan the next meeting.

(7) *Moving slowly but at the pace which the young people themselves set, begin to make plans for several weeks in advance, with the minimum of organization.* The election of officers can come much later. Begin to assemble some basic program material from your denominational bookstore or youth department.

Before too long, some attention should be paid to careful grading and age-grouping. The recommended divisions in the church are junior highs for ages 12-14, grades 7, 8, and 9; senior highs for ages 15-17, grades 10, 11, and 12; and older youth for those beyond 18 and out of high school.

JUNIOR HIGH

Because of the characteristics of junior high young people the church ministers to them in special ways. Their chief church experience ought to be in the Sunday morning church school class and the formal Sunday worship. Provision may be made for more informal activities at some other time in the week. Thus the junior high fellowship could be an extension of the church school class. Mixed boy-and-girl classes and units are recommended.

A variety of activities of short duration with emphasis on small-group relationships, should provide for the experiences of worship, study, play, and service. The best approach is to build a loyalty to group activities and to emphasize cooperative ventures. The junior high fellowship will do well with a simple organization, with officers elected for six-month terms to permit rotation among members. Leaders ought not to emphasize long-term committee or commission assignments, but depend upon total group concentration on the various program areas of the commission plan. This will certainly mean that junior highs are separated from the senior high young people, no matter how few are in either group.

Junior highs will need considerable adult guidance and leadership. Most material for this age-group is directed to the adult leader, and therefore the adults must prepare and direct the program. With coaching and encouragement, junior highs can prepare and present worship and recreation periods.

There are two strong recommendations at this point. Junior highs should not be sent to a youth rally away from home or on overnight and weekend retreats and outings. Most of these activities are planned for senior highs and older youth, and the junior highs will create the discipline problems. Though they may have fun, they will not gain much from the program. On the other hand, activities and functions designed especially for junior highs may be quite appropriate. Summer camps and conferences for junior highs are excellent.

Senior High

The dividing line between junior high and senior high has been generally established at the end of the ninth grade. However, the local school system will determine whether ninth graders should be classed with junior highs or with the senior highs. The group of senior high young people is probably the most important in the church. They are making life decisions which will affect their immediate future. They need the contact and fellowship of Christian people.

The first step is to make certain that a church school class for this age-group is available to all senior highs. They will make a conscientious group of pupils, able to carry their share of discussion and research. They should also be full communicant members of the church, and if they are not yet church members, immediate steps should be taken to prepare them for membership.

The senior high fellowship is apt to be the liveliest and most productive group in your church. Make sure that the junior high youngsters are removed, and provide the resources of adult leaders and printed material, a cheery room, and the open door.

With proper organization and coordination, the senior highs can maintain a satisfying year-round program. They will reach out to denominational, as well as interdenominational activities beyond the local church.

OLDER YOUTH

Our Protestant churches look after the young people who go to colleges and universities with a specialized campus ministry. But there are those who stay at home after high school graduation. Into many cities and communities, young people have come to work and study. Many of them look to your church for Christian fellowship. The local church in all fairness to the older youth must take the initiative in meeting their needs. At first glance, there may be only a few persons who might be reached. But once word gets out that a group of people are doing truly significant things, others will respond. A few basic principles might be stated here.

(1) *Older youth can be brought together on the basis of similar interests instead of age.* Such interests can be on the basis of work, or of hobby, or of background. There may also be a common need for recreational and social outlet, or a hunger for spiritual stimulation. Newcomers in the neighborhood, and military personnel stationed in nearby posts may desire church-related contacts.

(2) *Older youth can function in small groups.* Four or five persons can have a satisfying experience together pursuing their interests, and sharing their time.

(3) *Older youth are in a position to render many kinds of service in the name of the church.* These are people who have charm, time, money, and mobility, and a desire to be useful in the community. They possess talent and training in many fields.

(4) *While older youth need an adult adviser, such a person must have recognized status, intellectual and spiritual strength,*

maturity, and understanding. The role of this adult person is that of stimulator and coordinator, of inspiration and direction.

(5) *Any organization for an older youth group should be flexible.* They may meet for coffee on Sunday morning at the church. They may meet regularly or occasionally. They may specialize in service projects, office and clerical work for the minister, or sharing in a weekend work-camp downtown.

The possibilities are limitless. A little imagination, a survey of known personnel, a friendly session around coffee and dough-nuts, and a well-placed question can start the older youth going. More recently, older youth have been considered akin to the young adult in the life of the church. Since similar interests and not age bring these people together, the movement is toward placing the older youth in the young adult category. Whatever we call these persons, the church must extend its ministry to them.

CHAPTER EIGHT

Meaningful Activities

WHAT ARE the ingredients of an outstanding youth activity? Is there some formula which assures a good turnout, whole-hearted participation, satisfying public relations, and genuine fun? Do spiritual insights and understanding come from some rare moments in the church youth program? While the backbone of a good youth program is the week-by-week church school class and youth fellowship meeting, there are special activities from time to time that focus the energies of the young people. Let us consider some of these.

CHRIST'S WORKDAY

There are many factors which make Christ's Workday more than a money-raising event. Briefly, the young people of a local church agree to do odd jobs on a given Saturday, and give all earnings to a specified cause. Here are recommended steps:

(1) *The members of a church school class or a youth fellowship group must first become aware of a need to give a generous money gift.* This can well be a major project of the denomination, for its overseas or world service program, for a youth fellowship emphasis, or for any other legitimate and immediate situation.

(2) *The group then considers the possibility of designating a certain Saturday for a one-day workday.* All earnings are to be turned in for the agreed cause or the youth-giving plan of the church.

(3) *The young people commit themselves, as a group, to participate and to cooperate in the day's activities.* Those who hold regular jobs agree to contribute that day's pay. Others agree to accept odd jobs. The date is determined and announced.

(4) *An employment bureau is established.* By contacting adult members of the church, parents, relatives, and neighbors, the young people solicit work for the day. Depending upon the season, there are countless opportunities for work, both indoors and outdoors, for individuals, small groups, or the total group.

Suggested inside jobs include house-cleaning, furniture moving, ironing, baby-sitting, cooking, removing rubbish, clearing attic or basement, polishing silver, shining shoes, and other household tasks. Outside work includes washing cars, mowing lawns, raking leaves, gardening, landscaping, painting, changing screens to storm-windows, window-washing, removing summer furniture, cleaning garages. For many, there are errands to run, office and shop work. Young people in rural communities may find group jobs like gleaning corn, harvesting, major repairing or painting. Local situations will suggest other work.

It is not in the spirit of Christ's Workday to sell anything, whether it be candy or cake, or merely to receive a free-will offering. The unique feature is that every young person has worked for honest pay and given all earnings to the cause which the group has agreed to support.

(5) *Some very definite time, whether in church school class or evening meeting, is spent in studying the missionary project, the world service concern, the youth fellowship emphasis, or whatever the cause may be.* It is not always necessary that the earnings be given to a designated project; they may be applied against the local church's obligation to the denomination and its benevolent and mission budgets.

(6) *A final survey of jobs to be done and workers to be sent is made the week before the big day.* Direct and personal

requests for jobs have been more fruitful than distributing work-requests or by public announcements in church bulletins. A very helpful point is to specify a per-hour scale, or a per-job rate, keeping in mind that the work this day is honest work for reasonable pay. Many a young person has found a steady or repeat job by doing his task faithfully on the workday. The group agrees that over-payment and tips are to be refused.

(7) *On the morning of Christ's Workday, all the participants meet at the church for a brief and meaningful worship service.* This day is being set aside for the work of the church, and therefore God's blessing is asked for the efforts and contacts of the day. Young people can prepare and conduct this service.

(8) *Work assignments are distributed, and the workers are sent to their tasks.* If possible, young people ought to be sent out in pairs. If the jobs are scattered, advance arrangements for transportation need to be made. In fact, the whole day's activities need the guidance and coordination of the adult adviser to see that the process is moving on schedule. A roving adult, moving from job to job, can smooth difficulties and send reinforcement when necessary.

(9) *The noon meal can be picnic-style on the church grounds.* This gives opportunity for exchanging experiences and for reviewing the progress of the day. New work assignments are then made, and the afternoon shift gets under way.

(10) *The young people sometimes are guests at a spaghetti or covered-dish supper prepared by their parents that evening.* But even without such a supper, the young people come together for a social evening, and for a total evaluation session.

(11) *Finally, when all the earnings are submitted, including the money from those who worked at regular jobs, the gifts are dedicated at a special occasion,* during the church school or youth fellowship worship period, or as part of the regular worship service on Sunday.

While these steps outline the major processes, Christ's Workday becomes a significant experience for many reasons. First, the young people work as a group, and everyone shares in the excitement of the day. Then, there is a period of two to four weeks of anticipation and preparation which comes to a climax on the workday. The parents and adults for whom the young people work come to know at first-hand some of your young people. This is valuable public relations for the church. For the young people to give the day's earnings to a specified cause of the church becomes a lesson in stewardship, not otherwise learned. If the money goes to some missionary work of the church, there is valuable mission study involved. The money raised in such a manner will certainly be considerably more than the weekly accumulation of free-will gifts. Finally, the bond of Christian fellowship is strengthened by this day's experience.

The local church may make its own adaptations, of course, but we caution against frequent Christ's Workdays in any one year. While junior high young people may respond more wholeheartedly to this day, they will require more adult supervision.

PARENT-YOUTH SERIES

To provide an opportunity for better understanding between teenagers and their parents, the three-phase parent-youth series is recommended.

(1) *A fellowship evening constitutes the first phase of this series*. On a Sunday, the young people and their parents come together for a late afternoon vesper service. Leadership in the worship service may be shared by parents and young people. The service is followed by an informal buffet supper, with food brought by each family. There may be a few skits, some fellowship singing, and a funny story or two at the table.

A general discussion period in another room follows. The

topic can be any of the following: dating practices, hours to come home, use of the car, purchase of clothes, family chores, allowances, drinking, vocational preparation, or some other parent-youth concern. Any of these subjects can be discussed in a friendly, objective manner, which in a home situation may be emotionally upsetting.

To present the subject-matter, try role-playing or the use of some film or filmstrip. It is also possible to divide the parents and young people into buzz-groups, to identify the most pressing parent-youth problems. When all buzz-groups have reported, agree on the two or three items most frequently mentioned, for general discussion. The minister may be called on to make some concluding remarks, setting the problem in the light of the Christian message.

Move next into a period of group recreation. One of the parents or a parent-youth team may lead the group through some active and quiet games, ending with a friendship circle.

(2) *A work-night is the second part of this series.* There may be a major task in a general spring-cleaning of the church, some landscaping around the buildings, painting and repairing furniture, or other such jobs. Whether on a Saturday or an evening during the week, parents and young people are called together to join in this fellowship of work. There is no pretense at worship, or eating, or playing. The project needs to be cleared with the proper authorities, and adequate leadership should be provided.

(3) *The last of the three-phase series is a study night.* The recommended procedure is to divide the young people and their parents into clusters of four or five families, on the basis of geography, or of the age or school-grade of the young people. These family clusters meet simultaneously, preferably in homes, to study some specific area of Christian faith. For study material, the minister may preach a special sermon on a Sunday

morning, and provide discussion guides for each cluster. Perhaps some church school lesson may be reviewed and discussed. A chapter or two from a book, an article in some church magazine, or other sources may be used. One solid hour of intensive study on some aspect of Christian faith will be helpful to both parents and young people. An alternative to meeting in homes is for the whole group to meet at the church, see a film, or hear a presentation, and then meet in cluster groups in the church building, coming together again for review and evaluation of the discussion.

This is not a general family-night event, but limited to teenagers and their parents. Thus grandparents and kid brothers and sisters are not invited. All three parts ought to be done within a four-week period. To attempt to do all three in one week is ambitious. Advance notice of these dates should be announced so that parents may clear their calendars. While some parents may not be regular church-goers, their participation is nevertheless encouraged. Try the parent-youth series. It's dynamite.

YOUTH WEEK

One of the year's outstanding experiences for many churches is Youth Sunday. On this day the young people participate in the Sunday morning worship of the congregation, conduct the liturgy, offer prayer, read Scripture, and make brief presentations. Teenagers greet the worshipers at the door, sing in the choir, and generally assume full responsibility for the service. Such an occasion is a remarkable demonstration of youth's ability to lead in a significant worship experience. It binds the young people together in a common effort, and wins the admiration of parents and adult members of the congregation. More and more churches are observing Youth Sunday in cooperation with the Youth Week emphasis across the church.

The last Sunday in January to the first Sunday in February

has been declared Youth Week by the denominations cooperating in the National Council of Churches of Christ in the U.S.A. The youth arm of the National Council is the United Christian Youth Movement, which represents the youth fellowship organizations of the several denominations. By general agreement with the International Society of Christian Endeavor and of the UCYM, Youth Week has become an established event in the church year.

The last Sunday in January is "denominational Sunday," when the focus is upon the young people and their life in the local church. A common theme for the week is chosen by the UCYM. Resource material, posters, and leaders' guides are provided annually. Many denominations include the theme, the recommended worship service, and other features in their ongoing program.

The end of Youth Week, which is the first Sunday in February, is "community Sunday." In cities and town across the nation, young people of the cooperating churches come together for an impressive youth rally sponsored usually by the community's Christian youth council. The young people of your church should give support to this event. A community-wide youth rally alerts the young people to the fact that fellow-students in school are also active members in other Protestant churches. A demonstration of this type assures the community of the strength of Christian youth banded together for common witness.

Between the two Sundays there are opportunities for special study on the theme of the year, usually in cooperative efforts of the several denominations. Public presentations over the radio and television may be arranged. Well-planned exhibits, public demonstrations, and other events may be part of Youth Week. Some schools hold a religious emphasis week at this time. Capitalize on the many possibilities inherent in Youth Week.

PLANNING RETREAT

The alert youth group will set aside a weekend in the late summer to consider its hopes and dreams for the year ahead. Local resources will determine whether your teenagers can take over a campsite, somebody's lodge, a rural church, or a public park. It is advisable to go away from the home scene for this overnight planning retreat.

While facilities may restrict participation to youth officers, the more desirable situation is to encourage participation by every active and potential member of the youth program, both for church school and for youth fellowship functions. For an overnight occasion, we suggest that attendance be restricted to senior high young people.

Make clearance well in advance for the use of the grounds and facilities. Arrange for some adults to come along to prepare the necessary meals. Young people can help in the serving and dish-washing. Arrange for adult counselors on the ratio of one adult to every eight or ten teenagers. Make adequate provision for bedding and toilet facilities. Recreational activities and equipment should also be anticipated.

The main purpose of such a retreat should be clearly identified. While program-planning may be the chief purpose of the weekend, the retreat should serve to lead your officers, or your young people, into a sense of group unity. Allowing for times of group meditation, meals, and for group recreation, we suggest the following items for consideration at a planning retreat for a local youth group:

(1) *Review the experiences of the past year's program.* List the high points, the successes, the events that stand out. What were the factors which make them worth remembering? Likewise, what were some of the disappointing features of the previous year's activities?

(2) *Consider the hopes and dreams of your officers and members as they take stock of their present situation.* Are there

some conditions they would like to change? The time or place or frequency of the regular meeting, the manner and pattern of the worship and recreation, the irresponsible and unprepared youth leadership, poor attendance, the lack of spiritual grasp, the selfish attitude toward the missionary responsibilities of the church—these suggest the many items that may be discussed.

Try a "dream session" at this point. The total group is divided into small units of six to eight persons. Each group is asked to consider "How can we improve the youth program at our church?" Give them one hour, and list these rules:

• Let the suggestions come at random, out of the sky, in complete freedom.

• Don't be restrained in any manner. Everything is possible. Let no one say it's been tried before, or that there is no money for such activities.

• Build on the idea of another. Go hitch-hiking or piggy-back on suggestions already made. Really go wild.

• Make a long list. Be profuse and generous. Twenty to thirty new suggestions should come out of such a session.

• Then begin to pick from the list those ideas which can be used now. Select five or six of the "immediately possibles" and submit these to the total group.

• List on the chalkboard, or on the turnover chart, the "immediately possibles" from each group, and put them in priority order of attention.

(3) *Consider now the year's calendar.* Note the church holidays and seasonal events. Then include the special youth activities which were done in previous years, some of the ideas from the "dream session," also some major social events.

(4) *Review the resource materials for the year ahead.* This will mean the church school curriculum study books, the youth fellowship programs and topics, the new mission study books for the year, the denominational emphases and projects. Check

to see that subscriptions for appropriate youth magazines and reports to the denominational youth department are sent in.

(5) *Select now the topics which are to be discussed in the youth fellowship meetings in the months ahead.* There are several possible ways for doing this. One is to check again the list from the "dream session." Another is to list the areas of concern from the five commissions or program areas, and see how the young people react to each of these. It is also possible to run through the topics in the year's kit or book of programs, and secure an interest reaction to each topic.

Or this can be the time to divide the whole group into five or three sections, depending upon whether your youth fellowship uses the five or the three commission or program area grouping. Instruct each group to come forth with a recommended list of topics, sufficient for the necessary meetings in the year ahead.

(6) *Fit the selected topics into the year's calendar.* For each meeting and for each event assign a committee of three persons for preparation and presentation. They can, of course, bring more persons into their committee later. Or a commission (program area) may be similarly responsible.

(7) *Check to see that a balance is preserved.* Are all program areas well represented? Are the aspects of worship, study, service, and recreation in balance? How about types of meetings, the number of beyond-local-church contacts, social events?

(8) Finally, *identify one or two major objectives for the year ahead.* Will this mean doubling the attendance at youth meetings? A major dramatic presentation? Christ's Workday for the first time? Consistently effective meetings? An emphasis on spiritual commitment? Refer again to the "dream session" list for a possibility.

A weekend overnight retreat is most desirable. Every youth group, however, can spend at least one whole Saturday covering essentially the items indicated above. If at all possible, the meeting should be away from the home church. In any case, be sure to include in your youth program a session for long range planning.

YOUTH EVANGELISM

Four out of five teenagers in America are not actively related to the program of our churches. Far too many young people at the age of 14 or 15 years are lost from church schools. Where are the members of the scout troops, the basketball teams, and teen-towns that use our church facilities but do not share in the study, worship, and fellowship life of the church? Have we made an honest effort to reach the newcomers in our community?

Will your young people make a special effort to invite un-churched young people to worship, to study, and to share in the youth fellowship activities? If your youth officers and young people feel that a major effort in reaching out to inactive and non-churched persons is desirable, the following observations will be helpful.

Find out what help you can get from your denominational youth department or evangelism secretary. They may have a recommended pattern, with literature, packets, instructions, films, filmstrips, and other guidance material. It is possible that a united youth evangelism program will be held in your community in the months ahead. Check also with your congregation's evangelism committee. Do they put on an annual visitation evangelism program? How about doing the youth visitation at the same time?

Note also the two possible approaches in today's evangelistic program. One is to seek for immediate commitment to join the church, to profess one's faith in Christ, to secure a signed pledge that the person desires active relationship with a church. On the other hand, "fellowship cultivation" suggests that the visitor from the church ask a person to attend the regular worship services, invite him to join the church school class, and attend youth fellowship meetings. It may be suggested that later he may want to consider joining the church.

When these items are clearly understood, appropriate steps would be as follows:

(1) *Make a list of prospects to visit.* Review every possible source for names, such as church school rolls of several years past; church membership list, to note inactive persons; membership lists of groups and organizations using church facilities; lists of adult members of the church who have teenage children. Confer with the minister and get his suggestions. Let every youth member run through his lists of acquaintances, relatives, schoolmates, boy and girl friends, neighbors. Be especially alert for folks who have moved into the neighborhood recently. Don't overlook the physically handicapped, the shy and awkward who are apt to hide, and others who are so often ignored. Make a deliberate effort to invite the top-notch students and the leaders in school activities and athletics. And would your group dare cross color and class lines?

In some communities the churches cooperate with the high schools to secure a "religious preference" poll. Such records may indicate the names of students interested in a church of your denomination, and those who are not related to any.

(2) *Secure the commitment and promise of each of your young people to go out on the visitation program.* This will require orientation and training. With the printed helps made available from your denominational headquarters, and perhaps with invited leadership, your young people need to discuss the Christian necessity for reaching out to those not active and related to the church, to win others to Christ. The techniques of ringing doorbells, of coping with television and radio, of answering objections, of establishing a friendly attitude, of phrasing the invitation, and other details need to be practiced.

The best procedure at this point is to role-play a visit. Let the young people face up to many difficult situations, and evaluate their responses. Have enough persons take part so that the process becomes fairly well established.

(3) *Double-check with the minister, the church school superintendent, the adult advisers and others, alerting them to the possibility of increased attendance.* Let them know that the young people are going to make a special effort to bring new people into the life of the church.

(4) *In the schedule for the visitation program, arrange for a very special "friendship night" to which you will invite the newcomers.* This can be your regular youth fellowship meeting, dressed up with extra features to make them feel welcome and wanted. Check also that the date for your visitations does not conflict with other activities in the school or community.

(5) *The week before the visitation day, distribute pledge cards, instruction sheets, prospect cards, and some pieces of literature that may be left with the prospect.* Arrange also for transportation. Adult persons and parents may drive visitation teams from place to place, but in no event should they enter the homes. Team members should be matched, and visiting assignments should also be made at this time.

(6) *Your group might discuss the advisability of sending a friendly letter to each prospect a few days before the visitation.* In such a letter, indicate the hope of his joining the fellowship and sharing in the program of the church. List the particular class, group, and activity which are open for him. Announce that a visit will be made in the next few days. This letter may serve to start a favorable response, and actually open the way for a satisfying visit.

(7) *On the day of visitation, whether it be a Saturday afternoon, Sunday afternoon, or weekday evening, all young people ought first assemble at church for last minute briefing, and a*

worship moment of consecration. Before approaching each home, team members pause for a brief word of prayer for strength, guidance, and inspiration. Upon completion of their calls, each team reports its results at the church, or at a special report session for evaluation and sharing of experiences. It is possible that some second and third calls need to be made.

(8) *To make certain that those who agreed to come to church will actually do so, team members should call for the new-comers, and bring them along the first time.* The first experience at church is most difficult and crucial. Thereafter, make every effort to integrate them into the program.

While it is not possible to forecast the definite result of such a visitation program, one thing is certain: youth visitors who go out are immeasurably enriched, and their concept of the task of the church is learned anew. A youth-to-youth visitation evangelism program can well be an annual event.

SUMMER DOINGS

The alert church maintains a fairly active youth program during the summer weeks. While the pattern of regular weekly indoor meetings may be replaced with outdoor activities, a definite schedule and program should be outlined for the young people who will be at home. Allowing flexibility and last minute adjustment, these are among the many possibilities:

• An excursion of short or long duration, to some historic, denominational, or cultural center

• A series of house parties in members' homes

• A major work project in the community

• Entertaining young people from a church in another section of the state or environment (rural to urban, urban to rural)

• A visit and service project at a mission station or benevolent institution

• Some serious study of a mission book, Bible, or other resources

• House-to-house religious preference survey in new housing area
• A Lord's Acre project (planting, cultivating, harvesting a crop, the proceeds to go for church use)
• A local radio or television program
• Conducting a series of community outdoor vesper services
• Conducting play-time, story-time, and activity hours for neighborhood children
• Assisting in vacation church school and day-camp program

SPIRITUAL LIFE RETREAT

Senior high and older youth are capable of taking a con-centrated dose of religion. The years of church school classes, the pleasant experiences of youth meetings, the exhilarating fellowship of like-minded Christian youth, and the nurture of Christian family life can contribute to a new and vigorous search into the basic fundamentals of Christian theology. A spiritual life retreat can be sponsored by your church for your young people.

The time and place should suit local convenience. Certainly a weekend, starting with the Friday night meal, through Sunday afternoon, should be considered. A school holiday, the spring vacation, or other fortunate release from the school schedule may suggest a 48-hour block of time for such a retreat.

The place should be removed from the home scene. Depend-ing upon the season and the facilities, a likely place would be a campsite, a state park, a farmhouse, a cottage on the lake, river or sea, a rural church, or a summer home. You may find nearby a conference center equipped for a retreat experience. The idea is to find an isolated place free from public distraction, and away from the civilized and commercial world. Facilities for sleeping, eating, and meeting should be at hand.

Determine the general purpose of such a retreat. This is to be an experience of intensive study for personal spiritual enrichment. There will be moments of worship and inspiration. This is not a leadership training workshop, nor a program planning session. While there will be opportunity for limited recreation, this is definitely not a weekend party. It is also not a policy-making or legislative business meeting. The spiritual life retreat seeks to deepen the commitment of your young people.

It is highly desirable to protect every available moment for group study and activity. For this reason, meal preparation, serving, and dish-washing might be cared for by parents and adults who come along. Yet there is an undeniable fellowship in common work. A major physical work project has a valid part in a retreat experience of this type. Local facilities will again determine how this might be handled.

The question of who goes to the retreat must be clearly defined. At the least, the executive officers, cabinet or council members, chairmen of commission and program areas, should go. This may mean as few as five to ten persons. It is agreed in advance that all participants are of senior high age, or older. The next to be considered are members of the Christian Faith commission. Finally, attendance can be extended to all young people, both active and inactive. Full-time attendance and participation must be a definite rule. People who come late and leave early, and casual visitors, take away from the full value of disciplined, intimate, concentrated study. A special meeting of those who are going will help to set the tone, answer questions, and provide anticipation for the weekend program. The expense of this retreat is a valid and legitimate item on the church budget for youth work.

What then are some likely topics to be explored at such a retreat? From the wealth of possible subjects can be chosen questions like: What does it mean to be a Christian? What must I believe as a Christian? What does commitment mean to me? What is prayer? How can I serve the church? What is the grace of God?

To pursue any of these questions, several approaches are possible. A key-leader, whether drawn from within your congregation or from beyond the church, should make the major presentations and guide the discussions. Besides the straight lecture and group discussion are other possibilities including the use of audio-visuals, small-group discussions, problem-solving sessions, personal meditation, reading and research, intensive Bible study, prayer and worship. Consider the following tentative outline:

Friday evening: supper and fellowship singing
   General exploratory discussion on retreat theme
   Brief recreation period
   Moment of group devotion

Saturday morning after breakfast
   Brief devotions
   First lecture on theme; group discussion
   Bible study in small groups

Saturday afternoon
   Second lecture
   Small-group discussion
   Work project, or group recreation
   Personal reading, research, and meditation

Saturday evening
   Third lecture or film (or filmstrip)
   Group discussion
   Small-group prayer cell

Sunday morning
   Individual morning watch (devotions)
   Bible study in small groups
   Lecture and general discussion (or attend worship service in nearby church)

Sunday afternoon
  General evaluation session
  Consideration of back-home application
  Closing consecration service

One of the several valuable outcomes of the retreat may be the request to continue the small-group discussions from time to time. Thus a group of young people may agree to meet at regular intervals, perhaps the first and third Monday nights at the adult adviser's home, or at the homes of different youth members, for a specified one-hour session. Opening with prayer, the group may talk about current doings or problems at school, in the home, in the community. A period of Bible study or of prayer may be included. The discussion will always center upon the Christian implication and the need for deeper understanding and compassion.

Such a group, called a prayer cell, or fellowship cell, need not be large in number. If the group becomes more than ten persons, it should divide into two cells. One adult person should be present at each cell meeting. These cell experiences are intended to strengthen, not detract from, the regular program of the church. Nor are cell members to consider themselves an elite chosen group; an essential mark of the cell is humility.

Similarly, personal devotions can become a daily practice for these young people as another outcome of the retreat. Again, there may be requests for special Bible study, or for a class for those not yet received into full communicant membership.

Your church may join forces with the young people of one or two other churches in conducting such a retreat. Attendance then should be limited to a maximum of fifty persons. The ratio of adults to young people should be one to ten.

CHAPTER NINE

Beyond the Local Church

THERE ARE MANY relationships which involve young people, as individuals or as a group, beyond the local church. Some relationships are valuable and should be cultivated. Others must be studied and explored. Some involve responsibilities which must be faced.

THE DENOMINATION

Your young people belong to the denominational youth fellowship. This should be consciously and deliberately expressed in many ways. Does your church display the youth fellowship emblem or seal, in a poster, a felt banner, or some other way? Has your youth group "joined" the national fellowship and does it show a certificate of affiliation or membership to prove it? Do the members wear the fellowship emblem and carry membership cards?

In some instances, there is an obligation to support the regional or national youth program financially. Are you aware of your group's responsibility, and are you paid up in full? When periodic reports are requested, do you see that these are sent in to the proper office? Such reports are extremely helpful to your denominational leaders.

Are you aware of the several emphases and activities of your denominational youth program? For instance, do you use and read its publications? Are you supporting the mission study program? Do your young people give liberally in the recommended youth-giving plan? Do you know the youth delegates from your section to the most recent "national council" meeting of your denominational Youth Fellowship? What program activity did this national council recommend?

When did you last take your young people to a youth rally? The occasional gathering of young people of your denomination deserves complete support in attendance and participation. In the most simple situation, four or five neighboring churches may have a quarterly rally on a Sunday afternoon or evening. On the other hand, the number of churches and the area may be expanded to include 20 to 50 churches, with 100 to 500 young persons for an all-day Saturday meeting or a full weekend.

The denominationally sponsored youth gathering may be held under many names—rally, retreat, workshop, institute, meet, convocation, seminar, or conference. Its purpose can be one or several of these: information and instruction, study and education, worship and inspiration, legislative and policy-making, fun and fellowship, personal enrichment, leadership training. The meeting may be an annual, semi-annual, or quarterly affair. It may be open to all young people, limited to senior highs, beamed especially at youth officers, or limited to one or two delegates per church. Some meetings become traditional in time or place, and can then be included in advance planning of local youth fellowship programs.

Whether brief or long, small or large, the Christian youth rally, conference, or whatever, must demonstrate the highest expression of good programming. There must be proper sponsorship by an authorized group, to plan and conduct the affair. Adequate planning calls for long-range strategy, effective publicity, and careful consideration of details. A good meeting is organized around a central theme or purpose, provides inspiration and a renewed sense of belonging to a larger fellowship, informs and instructs about several phases of the Christian life.

The program may also provide interest groups to enrich the personal lives of teenagers. There is time for playing, eating, and singing. New friendships are made, horizons are widened, and denominational loyalty is strengthened.

At these large gatherings things happen that do not take place in the local church. Leadership is often of high caliber, latest resources are displayed, effective techniques are demonstrated, and ideas are exchanged. The meeting of new people, the exposure to higher standards, and the appeal for greater commitment have carry-over values for the local program. Since these larger meetings are designed primarily for senior high and older youth, do not send the junior highs. These younger people cannot comprehend the speeches or discussion and become easily restless. They may also become dissatisfied with this experience and therefore be unwilling to attend the functions really intended for them in their later teen years.

Check the summer camp and conference schedule of your denomination and urge your young people to share in this adventure. If possible, send a group of four or five, so that the stimulation and inspiration of the summer week can be brought back to the local group. Do not look for speeches or reports from these young people for having attended a conference or institute. Their deeper insight, renewed commitment, wider horizon, and new vision are not to be measured or weighed. Their influence will become evident in the weeks and months as they participate in planning and carrying on the regular program.

INTERDENOMINATIONAL

Your church demonstrates a united Protestant witness by joining forces with other churches in cooperative venture. There are many things which one church alone cannot do. The churches of the community need to meet occasionally in common worship of God, and to raise their collective voice in judgment of certain conditions in the community.

Young people, too, need to get the sense of united strength by pooling membership, leadership, resources, and facilities. For Protestant young people this is a way of making Christian fellowship real across denominational lines. Teenagers find a new regard for each other when they identify schoolmates with the Protestant churches in town. The cooperative work offers a wider scope of youth activity by opening doors to situations not available to an individual church. There is a more realistic Protestant approach to community problems as young people face current issues together. A united program can better meet the needs of all young people in the community. In fact, all the common experiences can strengthen the separate youth program of the local church.

An effective youth program at your church includes some interdenominational experience. At the community level, the cooperating churches can come together and sponsor Youth Week observances. The community worship service on the first Sunday in February can be the most likely function. A project or two may be undertaken, such as a vocations workshop, a family life institute, or a citizenship seminar. Because churches of other races may be involved, this will give added experience in harmonious race relations without calling attention to it.

Cooperative ventures can include a community survey, week-end work-camp, mission study pilgrimage, teen-town, summer recreation program, Easter sunrise service, and other activities appropriate for united sponsorship. Radio and television offer avenues of cooperative effort not available to one church. Public officials and institutions will grant privileges to representatives of an interdenominational group for interview, study, and research. A combined youth evangelism program, a religious emphasis week at the high school, some major service or work project in the community are other real possibilities for united action.

The place to look for guidance is the local council of churches or the ministerial association. Find out whether there is a committee on youth work already established. Perhaps there is a Christian youth council in existence. Use such established channels, and make it known that the young people in your church are anxious and willing to participate.

If there is nothing now in the picture, then responsible youth officers can propose an activity or function to be sponsored jointly by the young people of several churches. After one or two happy experiences, the organizations of the United Christian Youth Movement (UCYM) council can be considered and developed. In time, the UCYM council, representing the co-operating churches may sponsor one or more of the projects mentioned above.

The local UCYM council should secure the help of the county or state UCYM organization. This immediately relates your local movement to the county or state movement and opens other experiences and opportunities for your young people. These would include a big state-wide interdenominational conference, specialized seminars and institutes, and leadership training schools.

In the next larger sphere is the UCYM General Council which brings together representatives from the state UCYM organizations and from the denominational Youth Fellowships. Your young people thus have two major groupings which represent the concern and witness of Protestant youth at the national level. In addition, the youth-serving agencies related to the National Council of Churches are represented in the UCYM General Council. The UCYM is a movement of the youth of the Christian churches and related agencies, joined together by a common belief in Jesus Christ. In this unity, Christian youth face problems together and express their Christian witness at the local, state, national, and world levels.

To the Christian Endeavor movement goes the credit for pioneering in youth work. For almost a century Christian Endeavor societies in local churches across the nation and around the world urged greater participation and witness under the slogan "For Christ and for the Church." For their grasp of Christian faith and service, countless Protestant leaders are indebted to the Christian Endeavor emphasis on personal commitment and devotional practices. The weekly program using printed resources, with lay adult advisers, and age-group participation, have set the tone and pattern of much that we know today in the youth program. Through their rallies and conventions, Christian Endeavor societies have given leadership training and inspiration across denominational and racial lines.

The recent development of stronger denominational youth programs has affected some local churches which followed the Christian Endeavor program. Christian Endeavor still makes a significant contribution to Protestant church life, and cooperates with the United Christian Youth Movement.

YOUTH-SERVING AGENCIES

In the Christian education responsibilities of the local church, attention must be given to the role and relationship which youth-serving agencies have in serving children and young people. Because some of these agencies look to the church to sponsor local units and young people of the church often participate in the program offered by the agencies, some observations are in order.

Consideration is given to five national agencies which serve children and young people. In each instance, religious nurture and spiritual development are recognized as significant factors in personal growth.

The Boy Scouts of America provide a program to sponsoring institutions to use in achieving their own objectives in the character formation of youth. A sponsoring church operates its own scout unit, providing leadership, facilities, and funds. The three age-groups are Cub Scouts, ages 8-10; Boy Scouts, 11-13; and Explorers, 14 and up.

The primary purpose of Camp Fire Girls, Inc., is "to perpetuate the spiritual ideal of the home and to stimulate and aid in the formation of habits making for health and character." The program combines fun, friendship, achievement and ideals for girls in three age-groups: Blue Birds, 7-10; Camp Fire Girls, 10-15; and Horizon Clubs, 15-18. Sponsorship may be by individuals or institutions. A sponsoring church insures leadership, parental support, meeting place, and funds.

The purpose of the Girl Scouts, U.S.A., is "to help girls develop as happy, resourceful individuals willing to share their abilities as citizens in their home, their communities, their country, and the world." The Girl Scouts provide a leisure-time program in three age-groups: Brownie Scouts, 7-9; Girl Scouts, 10-13; and Senior Scouts, 14-17. Girl Scout troops are sponsored by organizations whose ideals and objectives are in accord with the Girl Scout movement.

The Young Men's Christian Association, while essentially a fellowship of men and boys, includes women and girls as members. The YMCA provides programs on four age-levels: Y-Indian Guides, fathers and sons, for boys 6-8; Gra-Y, for boys in grade school, age 9-12; Junior Hi-Y, for boys and girls 12-15; and Hi-Y for boys, Tri-Hi-Y for girls, 15-18. A church may sponsor any of these Y groups by providing a sponsoring committee, leaders, and facilities, and by recognizing both church and YMCA standards.

The Young Women's Christian Association has a teenage program called the Y-Teens for both girls and boys age 12-17. This program may include clubs, co-ed clubs, and other groups and activities, meeting in the YWCA, schools, and other community centers.

These five agencies are mentioned because they are associated with the National Council of Churches through a church-agency committee. They are a resource of the Christian education program of the church. Of the several advantages to the local church, the first is the opportunity to provide a character-building program for young people who live in the immediate neighborhood of the church. This of course will bring both members and non-members, the churched and the unchurched, into the activities of the week's program, and it may bring young people of other races and classes, and of other faiths. Thus the securing of additional members for the church and the church school may become possible. The major reason, however, for sponsorship of a group is the witness the church bears in showing concern for the weekday activities of growing youngsters.

There is undoubtedly wear and tear to the church property. Conflicts in schedule are also possible. A common problem is the weekend camping trip cutting into church school hours. Every assurance for mutual understanding should be established at the outset, and especially, it should be clear that this program is responsible to the Christian education program of the local church. In no event should a church permit its property to be used as a rented hall, allowing activities not consistent with the church's policies.

OTHER YOUTH MOVEMENTS

From time to time your young people may become aware of a sweeping religious "youth movement" involving students in the high school. This may be evident in Bible-carrying students, a Friday night house party, a big Saturday night rally, devotional groups at school, and other manifestations. Some movements may use films, radio, and television while others may depend on a series of printed resources, meetings, and parties. Generally these movements are noted for their attractive personalities, professional-looking literature, extensive camping program, and considerable Bible study. Much reliance is placed on winning the school hero of athletic or student council fame.

There apparently is a wealth of funds and support for their program.

The local church youth worker should study each incident with considerable care. Points of caution include these: What is the theology that is being taught? Is what the movement teaches consistent with your church's tradition and understanding? What attitude do its leaders have concerning the established church? What follow-up does the program provide for those they touch emotionally and spiritually?

The denominationally-based youth program seeks to strengthen the relation between the growing teenager and his local church. Anything which disrupts this relationship must be viewed with concern. While no Protestant church or denomination claims to have all the answers, certainly responsible congregations can provide an adequate program and do an effective job in seeking lives committed to God.

Some commercial publishing houses that provide Sunday school literature have moved into the youth group realm. Local churches not aware of the implications permit their young people to undertake such a program. The questions raised above are also pertinent here.

THE COLLEGE STUDENT

Your church will send an increasing number of young people to colleges and specialized schools beyond high school graduation. These students enter a world of relative freedom, intellectual stimulation, moral dilemma, and vocational choice.

The wise church will begin early to help prepare its young people for this transition. Such preparation includes basic understanding of the purpose of life, of a sense of vocation, of the need for disciplined study, of the choice of appropriate school, and of the stewardship of time and opportunity. There are, in addition, such simple things to anticipate as how to write letters home, what to do with free time, how to make friends, how to handle money, and the like. Some more difficult decisions will have to do with gambling, drinking, carousing, foul talk, and for some, smoking. The gamut of boy-girl relations needs to be faced: how to get a date, necking and petting, the question of getting married while in school. Certainly the possibility of marriage with one of another faith should be considered.

Undergirding all must be a sustained conviction of one's faith, a positive attitude to the church, and a conscious dependence upon God. In this process of preparation, the church can aggressively counsel its young people individually and collectively, toward decisions about vocation and school.

Your young people who leave for college still look to your church as home base. Establish some pattern to remember these students with frequent messages and correspondence. Be alert to the weekends, holidays, and vacations when the young people come home, and involve them in your church activities. Probably your greatest task is to impress upon each person that his first objective is to be a student, and second, to be a Christian student. Demonstrating his Christian faith while being a student has implications beyond the surface act of attending church on Sundays. From the basic decision never to cheat, to the more strenuous and intense search for knowledge and integrity, your student indeed is a witness to the God of love and the God of truth.

Insist that your student relate himself to a church on or near the campus for worship, study, and fellowship. He will probably find other students at this church, and perhaps a fellowship especially for students. In addition, he should look for a campus Christian fellowship. Such a group may have a denominational label, or it may be a more inclusive Christian association, or a student Christian fellowship or foundation. Have him meet the adult adviser or religious counselor, who may be known as campus pastor, chaplain, minister to students, or faculty adviser to the campus Christian group. Urge his participation in the fellowship and activities of such a group with the reminder again, that his first responsibility is to study.

Similar counsel in varying degrees can be given to those who enter nursing school, business college, trade institutes, and other specialized schools. Because these schools are often found in metropolitan centers, more help must be given to relate such students to nearby churches and their fellowship groups.

For the student who commutes to school from home, the basic relations between local church and campus life must be reviewed with care. The fact that he is a student comes first, and his need of a student fellowship comes next. In relation to these needs he can then consider his church relationship with its necessary responsibilities. In any event, the local church should give continuous guidance to its students away from home.

MILITARY PERSONNEL

We are living "in an age of peril, a time of tension and watchfulness." This observation by the President of the United States indicates vividly why ten years after the second world war some 3,500,000 persons are still in United States uniform. Slowly and reluctantly the American way of life is adapting itself to this military concept. Without yielding its tenets and beliefs about the sanctity of life, the Protestant church must reckon with the fact that its young people face two or three years of military training.

The responsible church will provide an adequate ministry to those in uniform. They are usually between the ages of 18 to 21, half of them overseas. Many of them are married, and may have children. All the preparation that has been suggested for the college student must be provided, with greater stress. The men and women in military service make a sharper break from civilian life than does the college student leaving home. The temptations of liquor, sex, and gambling are compounded with homesickness, loneliness, inactivity, and strange surroundings. The regimentation, routine, lack of privacy, low moral tone, and the cynical attitude combine to disillusion the church-sheltered youth in a new military situation.

In anticipation of this kind of life, several general approaches might be made. First is the preparation of all young people for understanding the nature of our military position, our nation's foreign policy, our church's attitude regarding military issues, and youth responsibility. Some honest discussion of all these matters would be helpful. For the individual who is facing induction, personal counseling with the minister and a Christian adult with military experience is recommended. The several possibilities before him, concerning work and college, marriage and military service should be seen in relation to each other.

There are ways in which the local church can maintain a meaningful contact with those in uniform. This can begin with a special service of recognition and dedication at church on the last Sunday before leaving. A significant gift will be welcome. At the actual departure, the presence of church people and young folks at the bus or railroad depot will attest to the loving relationship and prayer which go with him. Constant correspondence and remembrance from the church and its members are essential. Whenever he comes home, make special effort to include him in the ongoing program of the church. If your church is located near a military post or camp, a warm and open welcome to visiting servicemen ought to be provided. If possible, integrate them into the church program.

The United Fellowship of Protestants is the youth fellowship in the naval installation, military camp, or air base, stateside, afloat, and abroad. Advise your youth member of this organization, provide a letter of recommendation to the chaplain, and urge him to relate himself to the Protestant group wherever he is. The United Fellowship is informal, flexible, and fluid. There may be opportunity to sing in the choir, help with the worship, conduct church schools, and participate in fellowship activities similar to those in the home church. The big difference is that the personnel will be coming and going, with rapid turn-over, necessitating continual change in the nature of the program.

The possibility for witnessing to the Christian life is immense and difficult. The greater possibility is that the temptation for the easy life will turn your youth away from the church. Your efforts to sustain their faith and convictions are doubly essential.

THE UNCHURCHED

In the light of the great commission entrusted to the church how can we justify the casual and indifferent manner in which we minister to young people? Too easily we permit our teenagers to slip away from the church. We are content to work with the faithful few. We blame the school, the community, commercial recreation, parents and others for claiming the time and loyalty of our adolescent population. We see them in hordes at the high school. They hang around at the favorite joints. They converge at the dances. Probably some of them are of the undesirable elements—the fringe, junior hoodlums, the delinquents, and perhaps we pass them off as non-joiners, anyway.

The fact remains that the church is responsible for ministering effectively to all teenagers, churched and unchurched. A basic study of your program would include a survey of your membership personnel. How many teenagers do you have in church school, evening fellowship, church worship? How many children of adult members are teenagers? Consider then those who have dropped out of active relationship from church school and church membership, but are still living in the neighborhood. This group of teenagers is your potential, for whom your church is immediately responsible.

Your survey next covers the program you provide for this "potential." Do you have attractive and able adult workers?

Are you prepared to take all of the young people into your church school? How are you providing for their varying interests? Are the fellowship groups open to all? Do you have a challenging, balanced program?

Consider now the young people who are known to be unchurched in your community. Have they ever been approached, as individuals or as groups, to share in the life of the church? Have your young people ever attempted a youth evangelism program to reach them? How is your church following up newcomers in the neighborhood? Do you scan the membership of the club groups and agencies which use your facilities for possible contact? Do your own young people have friends and acquaintances who might be integrated into your program? Are you avoiding the race issue?

What might a church do to reach the unchurched? One possibility is to open your social hall for recreation purposes. Where there are no other facilities in the neighborhood, a teen-town may be the answer. If your church has gym facilities, would you sponsor a basketball league? If your church has access to a camp-ground, would you schedule a program there including the unchurched? How about dramatics, hobbies, music, crafts, hot-rods, and other interest groups to bring them under church influence?

A thorough survey of this type may call for cooperative action of the churches in the community. It may reach into the high school for participation in some religious emphasis week. It may call for joint sponsorship of teenage activity. Surely it will call for adult guidance and supervision.

This is not primarily an effort to combat delinquency, or to keep young people off the street, or to win converts. An outreach to the unchurched is to extend the Christian gospel and the Christian fellowship to growing teenagers. They need spiritual stimulation and daring experiences to know and acknowledge Jesus Christ as Savior and Lord. No effort must be spared in being aggressive at this point.

The Broadcasting and Film Commission of the National Council of Churches seeks to reach the unchurched by means of radio and television. The increasing use of television will mean that local churches need to anticipate newcomers who may peer cautiously into church doors. Television can stimulate an interest in the spiritual life and raise new hope in the hearts of people. But they need the fellowship of Christians to nurture and sustain this faith. Be alert therefore for the television programs sponsored by councils of churches, and especially those beamed at young people by the Broadcasting and Film Commission. The CBS-TV show Look Up and Live, which appears on Sunday mornings, has had unusual response in its weekly presentations aimed at unchurched youth.

CHAPTER TEN

Where Do We Get Help?

WHILE IT IS possible for youth leaders to plan and pursue their youth program without any outside help, the wise person will look into the many resources available to make him a better leader. In this instance, and throughout this book, the word "resource" refers to the material, people, experiences, and places which increase our usefulness as adult workers, enrich our program, and provide additional help and stimulation for our task.

PRINTED RESOURCES

The first awareness you should have is that your church belongs to or is affiliated with an established denomination in this country. You have access to a library of material provided especially for you and your young people. Indeed, you are the customer for whom the books, magazines, and other literature are written. Your proper use of them is intended to make your work more effective.

There are many publishing houses and bookstores which provide a variety of literature useful in our churches across the land. For many good reasons you should give prior consideration to the resources of your own denomination. The reasons include the concern for an adequate theology, a sound educational and psychological approach, comprehensive progression through the ascending age-groups, and your denomination's contribution to the life and work of the church within and beyond the nation. Not the least of these reasons is the financial support which your purchase and use of these materials provide for your denomination.

(1) *Church School Curriculum.* You will ordinarily find two types of church school material. The international uniform series seeks to provide Bible-centered lessons, placing emphasis upon the content of the Bible record. Thus a common scripture lesson is used in all age-groups in the church school, with appropriate adaptation and approach to each age-group. Representatives from thirty denominations prepare the outline, the themes, and the selections of the scripture lessons. Coordinated and simultaneous study of the same Bible lesson on a given Sunday across the nation in all age-groups is thus made possible. Each denomination, however, prepares its own lessons, giving its theological interpretation and denominational emphasis.

In addition, most major denominations produce a series of lessons which are life-centered, observing the same general theme for the several age-groups, and seeking Bible truths for guidance. Such a series seeks the cooperation of the home and parents, and attempts more varied approaches in teaching methods. It would be good for you and the other teachers of young people to be alert to the possible alternative series available to you through your denomination. Deliberately and knowingly decide which series you wish to use. In making such a decision, it is more important that the same series is used throughout the church school to maintain continuity and consistency in religious teaching, than to permit teachers and departmental superintendents to go off on various tangents to suit personal whims.

(2) *Youth Fellowship Topics.* Whether it comes in a quarterly or monthly magazine, a series of booklets, or a kit volume, the youth department of your denomination publishes or provides a set of program suggestions for your evening youth

fellowship groups. You will find these topics have been carefully planned, thoughtfully written, and often integrated into the ongoing life of your denomination. There is also timely use of mission study emphases, the Youth Week theme, and national and international situations. These topic materials make a valuable cumulative library.

Most topics are written to provide background information, an approach to a subject matter, recommendations of other resources such as books and visual aids, and possible related activities. Basic instructions are suggestive in each instance; the young person or the planning committee must make adaptations of the material for the local situation. How the material is used, what additional resources are introduced, the worship to introduce or close the discussion, and other possibilities should be determined by your young people. Discourage direct reading from the printed pages; urge instead the use of language normal to your group.

Good material will probably require more time in preparation than poor material. Good material will call for considerable struggle to think out the situation, to explore a real problem with the young people, to instill the need for some suitable follow-through action. The big problem for your youth leader is to conduct an effective discussion. This knack comes with trial and error, and the adult leader must be patient and encouraging.

Often the recommended topic material is discarded or bypassed as not appropriate, too difficult or time-consuming in preparation. The maturity of your young people may not be as advanced as that expected in the printed material. The fact remains, unless your young people and the adult worker take the time to digest the material, introduce local and current example, and make other adaptations for your group, the use of any printed topic material is not worth the time and effort. To sit down and stand up according to the instructions in a "canned" program adds nothing to the growth of your young people. Only with struggle through frustration does honest growth take place.

(3) *Youth Fellowship Handbook.* Check with your denomination's youth department on the latest and appropriate handbook, manual, notebook, or other printed guidance material intended for the young people and their leaders. Such handbooks describe in detail the purpose, the organization, the emphases, and relationships recommended for the youth fellowship group. Valuable hints, suggestions, instructions, and information are usually included.

In many instances each program area of the commission plan is described in detail, together with a number of program and project suggestions. The particular concerns and interests of your denomination are emphasized, and your young people are encouraged to observe them. In addition to the handbook, your denomination and its youth department may offer other materials for the strengthening of your youth program. Take advantage of this service.

(4) *Story Papers and Magazines.* Some denominations make available a series of story papers and magazines, either separately or together for junior high and senior high young people. These publications may come weekly, bi-weekly, or monthly. They are intended to supplement the church school and youth fellowship material, to entertain, inform, and stimulate the young people in personal reading. Sometimes there are devotional helps and personal enrichment articles. Are you securing denominationally produced and recommended material of this type for your young people?

(5) *Leaders' Helps.* Practically every denomination has a monthly or quarterly magazine directed to church school teachers and adult workers with young people. While these magazines may have an over-all approach, there are usually articles

and discussions of particular concern to junior high and senior high teachers and advisers. Insist on having your personal copy, and establish a library of these magazines over the months and years.

The *International Journal of Religious Education* is the official publication of the Division of Christian Education of the National Council of Churches of Christ in the U.S.A. This monthly magazine is recommended for the treatment of subject matter by nationally known leaders in the various fields, including working with young people.

(6) *Youth Department Releases.* Your denominational youth department may release a leaflet from time to time, which keeps you abreast of emphases and development of the denomination's youth program. This publication may be directed to your youth leaders for their guidance and direction. There are also regional youth offices which publish newsletters and bulletins.

(7) *Your Bookstores.* Your denomination has one or more bookstores to serve your needs. If they publish a catalog, have one at hand. At least, know where your denominational bookstore is located and learn to use its services.

(8) *Councils of Churches.* Your state council of churches, the United Christian Youth Movement, and even perhaps your local council office offer guidance and material for local church groups.

(9) *Songbooks and Devotionals.* Do you know whether your denomination provides a fellowship songbook and daily devotional booklet? Get and use them.

AUDIO-VISUAL RESOURCES

The increasing use of audio-visual resources reflects the church's awareness of this new tool for improving our teaching and training program. The most common of these are the 16 mm. sound films, of varying lengths, in many titles, on many interests. The films come in color, or in black and white.

There is also the filmstrip, which is a long strip of one-picture shots, projected on the screen, one frame at a time. These pictures may be drawings, art work, cartoons, or live photographs. These too may come in color or black and white. While the picture is shown on the screen, an accompanying script may be read. The sound filmstrip comes with a phonograph record carrying the words, accompanying music, and other sound effects.

It is possible to secure a set of slides on many subjects. These slides can be assembled also from private collections, and thrown on the screen much as albums and snapshots are shown to friends. Flat pictures are helpful in depicting the subject under discussion. It is also possible to secure records of music, drama, or narration.

Since these resources are the principal tools generally available and used by church groups, you should know your most convenient audio-visual library. The most likely place to look is your denominational film library. This may or may not be associated with the denominational bookstore. Perhaps the Religious Film Library has a convenient branch office. The film libraries of other denominations than your own should also be considered.

In many metropolitan areas there are commercial film rental services which increase the range of titles and subject matter for your use. The extension services of many state universities offer rental privileges, as do the film departments of the municipal libraries across the nation. Become acquainted with these libraries.

To secure films, filmstrips, slides, records, and other audio-visual pieces, you should first assemble the catalogs from as many of these libraries as you can. Some release annual catalogs, or a basic catalog with annual supplements. The most comprehensive catalog for church use is probably the *Audio-Visual Resource Guide*.

You should have access to the necessary projection equipment for the 16 mm. sound film or the filmstrip, a three-speed record player, and a screen adequate for the size of room and audience. If your church has an alert audio-visual committee, they may own all the basic equipment, together with a library of filmstrips. Learn to use the equipment with ease and confidence, and train some of your young people to this task.

The selection of the title of the film, filmstrip, record, or other tool should be determined by the theme or topic to be presented. Then, having your immediate need in mind, scour the catalogs for the treatment most suitable for your situation. Use the projected picture as your tool, and really use it. Do not permit yourself to be trapped into getting a title because it comes without cost, or someone thrusts it upon you. Be positive that the item is of your choosing. Of course, it is helpful to receive recommendations, and to note the commentary which goes with the selection. Watch carefully to see whether this particular piece is suitable for the intended age-group.

When you have determined the choice of your particular film or filmstrip from the catalog, send in your request early, giving the title, the date when you wish to use it, and your name and address. It is recommended that you give one or two alternate titles and one or two alternate dates, so that your request can be properly honored. You will receive a confirmation note as soon as your request is received.

Upon arrival of the film or filmstrip, check immediately to see that you received what you wanted. Together with the planning committee for the evening's meeting, preview the film, running through the leader's discussion guide, and become comfortable in its use. Check all equipment once again before the actual meeting, after setting the screen and projection equipment in place.

If the filmstrip requires a reading script, have the reader run through the script, together with the projected frames of the filmstrip, so that the coordination will be smooth. Check the record player for volume and sound, for proper location, and for necessary additional extension wire. Try to attain almost professional timing in the projection of the first frame before dimming the house lights, with record player previously warmed up for immediate use. Assign different persons to each task, so that the discussion leader will be freed from mechanical responsibilities.

We must remind ourselves again that the use of audio-visuals is to assist us in bringing the subject in a vivid form, in color and sound, in nearness and drama, in overwhelming reality into our midst. We would be misusing audio-visuals if we used them as time-killers in a program, or as entertainment, and at best, as perhaps "educational." Bend the use of the audio-visuals to your purpose, to help present the subject matter more effectively.

A few words of explanation are required before the pictures are projected. Inform the audience of the nature of the story, suggest that certain personalities or incidents be watched, and propose one or two basic questions which will be asked as soon as the projection is completed.

At the end of the projection, the house lights should go on promptly. Before the projector lights are dimmed, and before too much confusion sets in, the discussion leader may pose the basic question again. The use of chalkboard or turn-over sheets helps carry the discussion along. Try to focus attention, not on the technical error or skill in the photography or art work, but on the implications and incidents reflected in the story. Make frequent reference to the picture personalities by name. Pursue the discussion as far as is necessary, and to the desired conclusion.

Upon adjournment, restore the rented material to the proper container, enclosing the supplementary pieces which came along, and mail these immediately to the film library. This is courteous and proper. Honor and pay all bills promptly.

While films and filmstrips aid tremendously in understanding our community and its many problems, we would fall into bad habits if we relied on audio-visuals as an alternative to other possible methods of topic presentation. Our young people are bombarded with audio-visuals through the theaters, television, and in school. They are therefore highly critical, not only of the choice of the title, but of the use of the medium.

PERSONAL RESOURCES

In every congregation and community are a number of persons who can make valuable contributions to your youth program. To tap this reservoir of talent, the planning committee for the church school class or youth fellowship meeting should be thoughtful in extending invitations. The wise and occasional use of parents, members of the congregation, and other persons in the community to give added insight to the program may greatly enrich the class session and the evening meeting.

Invited persons should be used to strengthen the specific program emphasis you have in mind. What peculiar contribution can this speaker bring? What background and experience may make his presence uniquely helpful? How will he stimulate your young people, and what are the possible end results of his coming? The wrong way to use the invited guest speaker is as entertainer or as someone to fill a gap in the program. The danger is to depend upon the one person to carry the evening's program or the class session. While this is possible, and the speaker may cherish this opportunity, the welfare and direction of the youth program should be the main consideration.

Having agreed that a certain person can make a valuable contribution in the understanding of a particular subject, he should be invited early. Once the date is confirmed, it is advisable to have a personal conference with him, outlining the reason why he is invited, his special role, the sequence of events before and after his coming, and the full program of the class or meeting when he is present. In this personal conference, or by correspondence, clearly determine the topic or theme, the general scope of his discussion, and the desired outcome that you have in mind. Suggest a time limit for his participation, and let him know what type of discussion period you plan to have following his talk. If he comes from a distance, or if he is a professional speaker in any sense, you should have an understanding concerning his expenses and honorarium in advance. Double-check his transportation arrangements. On the appointed day or hour, be sure to have two young persons assigned to welcome him, to look after his welfare, and to be his companion and guide during the meeting. Make him feel at home, and urge his participation in as much of the meeting as possible.

To make his presentation most effective, arrange some definite plan of discussion which will follow immediately. Here are some possibilities:

(1) *Have a panel of three or four previously chosen to frame some questions to be asked.* Let each panel member present his question, until all questions are in the open. Then ask for additional questions from the audience.

(2) *Divide the total audience into "listening groups," and assign a question to each group in advance.* Immediately upon the completion of the talk, each listening group may discuss the question and raise others.

(3) *Have the total audience go into six-minute six-man buzz-groups* to consider what was said, directing their conversation to one specific question which was previously agreed upon with the speaker. Let each group then report its findings, permitting the speaker to make observations on these reactions. Or each buzz-group can determine what one question to put to the speaker.

(4) *Invite the speaker to meet with a small committee or with the officers,* to secure his evaluation concerning a certain project or program emphasis that is in the schedule ahead. His remarks may suggest new ideas for further exploration.

These suggestions indicate how you may make maximum use of the invited person. It is worth repeating that in all fairness to the speaker, and to your young people, anything less than this is an insult to him and to your group. The worst offense is to invite a person to speak on anything he desires. This proves that your group looks upon him as nothing more than a time-filler, and that your program sequence is of little substance.

LEADERSHIP TRAINING FOR ADULTS

The conscientious adult worker, whether church school teacher or adviser to the youth fellowship group, will make every effort to increase his usefulness by taking leadership training courses available to him. In practically every community there is at least one leadership training school for every church each year. Such schools may be sponsored by a council of churches, a ministerial association, a group of churches, or even by one large church. Some training situations are provided by denominations, at the local or the regional level, and occasionally by state and national leaders. These training opportunities usually include a section or class for leaders and teachers of young people. On occasion, the whole training experience has to do with various phases of the youth program.

There may be summer opportunities lasting one or two weeks. Some schools carry their program for six weeks, one night a week. Others may do their work over a weekend, or perhaps the major part of one day. Hardly ever can you expect to get a fair treatment of leadership training in one or two hours. If you find that in your situation there is really no opportunity to secure specialized guidance, you could properly appeal to your minister to arrange for some outside guidance and instruction.

While adult workers may feel the need for knowing methods and techniques, it is also important that every adult person increase his personal grasp of the Christian faith. Special study at the church, or beyond, should be a part of his schedule. A youth work institute, a demonstration school or workshop for adult leaders of youth, a leadership training school, and many other gatherings of youth leaders are taking place throughout the year, in all parts of the country. Be specially alert to these opportunities, and make every effort to share in one each year. The wise church will provide a budget item to cover registration, transportation, and other expenses for this purpose.

Perhaps the greatest revelation for an adult worker who attends a leadership school is the satisfying fact that he belongs to a company of those who face similar frustrations and problems. A spirit of kinship in working with Christian youth is developed, and each person contributes out of some high, or low, experience. To employ this bond of common effort as a basis of strength, we suggest the "cluster plan."

Some four or five churches closely situated, whether of one or of several denominations, commit themselves to send all adult workers with young people, church school teachers, youth fellowship advisers and others, to an occasional supper meeting. The purpose of such a meeting is to focus on one phase of the youth program, and then to consider its application in the churches represented. Presumably, there is no outside expert or leader brought in. It is possible that only one or two of the ministers may be present. Essentially this is a fellowship of adult workers who look unto themselves for direction and inspiration.

This sharing experience will be of special help to new teachers and advisers of young people. Resource material, discipline problems, a successful project, some neighborhood personality, a local crisis, and other items may come up for conversation while the evening moves on. There need be no formal or official organization. Perhaps two such meetings each year would be sufficient. Establish dates, and the church where each meeting will take place. Let the host church entertain in rotation. While the personnel may change from meeting to meeting, the meetings would provide a continuous source of strength for all adults who serve the church young people of the neighborhood. To institute this cluster plan, the initiative may be taken by the adult workers of one church, or the plan may arise in a conversation with two or more ministers.

Here is a list of suggested items for discussion at these cluster sessions:

Understanding young people

Review of recommended topic material for youth fellowship meetings

Evaluation of junior high and senior high church school curriculum

Goals of Christian education for youth—junior high, and senior high

How do youth learn?

How use drama?

Resources for audio-visuals, how use?

Questions youth ask on religion, how answer?

Discipline, how to secure

Irresponsibility, dependability, punctuality

Increasing participation, attendance, and interest

Work projects? Money-raisers?

What is stewardship for young people?

Effective mission study

Persons, agencies, industry, and civic resources for youth program

How deal with community recreation, boy-girl problems?

Is delinquency or vandalism present in the community?

How improve parent-church relation?

What is value of summer church camp and conference program?

What makes a good youth rally?

How can we participate in interdenominational activities?

What must we do to grow spiritually ourselves?

To increase your grasp of the role of the church, of Christian faith, of Christian education, and of youth work resources and techniques, the minimum leadership training program for each adult worker and teacher should include these elements:

(1) Read a book each year on some phase of Christian education, Christian faith, missions, or youth work, for general personal enrichment.

(2) Attend once a year a workshop, institute, demonstration school, laboratory, conference or retreat for adult workers of youth.

(3) Keep abreast of denominational printed resources.

(4) Maintain faithful and active relationship to the life of the home congregation, and personal discipline (private devotions and prayer).

(5) Have access to a growing library of youth work material.

(6) Meet regularly with a group of adult workers of youth, either in one's own church, or from a group of neighboring churches.

(7) Become expert in some phase of the youth program, such as program planning, recreation leading, worship resources, mission study, and so on.

LEADERSHIP TRAINING FOR YOUNG PEOPLE

Your young people who hold leadership responsibilities need help and stimulation. While there are some individuals who seem to possess innate traits of leadership, there is nevertheless a whole realm of youth fellowship methods, materials, resources, emphases, and standards which must be learned. Apart from personal observation and adult encouragement, the young person might look to these other possibilities:

During the summer weeks, your denomination conducts a number of camps and conferences designed for young people, often restricted to age-groupings of junior high, senior high, and older youth. While the trend is to tone down the emphasis for specific leadership training, there are enough elements in the usual one-week program to constitute a valuable experience for budding youth leaders.

Periodically, your denomination may sponsor a major conference or convention during the summer weeks. This large gathering may provide special sections for youth leaders, on different subjects, for different age-groups.

The United Christian Youth Movement, on the state and regional basis, conducts a series of one-week training conferences every summer. Secure the schedule for your area and send your youth leaders to it. During the school year your local or state Christian youth council may hold a conference, rally, or other functions.

Practically every church belongs to an association or convention, regional, synodical, state, or other groupings of denominational youth fellowships, which hold an annual or semi-annual weekend institute, retreat, conference, or rally with leadership training in mind. In some instances such meetings may be specifically geared to one of the five program areas, or even more narrowly pointed within the program area. A creative arts workshop, a recreational laboratory, a spiritual life retreat, a mission institute, citizenship seminar, family life institute, an officers' retreat, and other situations are bound to come within reach of your church from time to time. The alert church and its adult workers will make certain that its youth leaders take advantage of these opportunities. Again, scholarship funds may be set aside to encourage attendance and participation.

On occasion, you and your church may invite a group of youth leaders to come to your church, spend a day, weekend, or week with your young people. Their chief function would be to stimulate, interpret, and encourage the best in youth activities, to show that church work is fun, that there are many possibilities and varieties of program and activities, and to open the eyes of your young people to the wider horizons from which these visitors come. These youth leaders may come as a deputation team from a college campus; they may be officers and leaders of the youth cabinet of your regional or sectional denominational youth fellowship; they may be a summer caravan team; they may have other relationships and responsibilities in your denominational youth program.

Your church may also have access to the service of professional or semi-professional field workers, assigned to the state or national youth departments, to visit and counsel with you and your youth leaders. These persons, too, may come for an evening, a day, several days, or a week, depending upon their functions, to serve your church.

For those churches which might encourage in-service training, or apprenticeships of young people, the pattern of appointing specialists for the year is suggested. Taking, for instance, the field of worship and recreation, select two young persons for each realm, and let them know that they are expected to serve as specialists and resource persons for the year ahead. Send them to summer training opportunities, provide adequate printed resources, and give them special adult help. Make them proficient in their field. Insist that they maintain high standards of programming in their field.

Thus, for a given youth fellowship meeting two young persons are assigned to the worship specialists with whom they plan the worship segment of the evening's program. While the plans are being worked out the specialists suggest new and varied possibilities, making certain that the best elements of worship are conserved. In this planning moment, the specialists suggest material, hymns, readings, and arrangements to avoid a weak pattern. In this process, duplication and similarity of presentation will be avoided over a period of weeks.

Similarly, two young persons are assigned to the recreation specialists to plan the recreational part of the evening meeting. The plans are reviewed, games suggested and listed, new activities are introduced, and a wider range of experiences is provided through this exchange. The actual leading of the games and recreation will be done by the persons responsible for the evening, but the specialists will participate with the total group. They will make their own evaluations from week to week.

In this manner, for every meeting, two new persons are given the advantage of the accumulated experiences of the two youth specialists, in both the worship and recreation fields. In time, every person will have had this advantage. These specialists should be chosen from among the young people. They may be the chairman of the Faith Commission, or of the Fellowship Commission, or other young people, selected for their interest and proficiency in the field. A new set of specialists might be appointed each year. This pattern might prevail in other areas of the youth program, such as in discussion techniques, use of audio-visuals, and so on.

EQUIPMENT AND FACILITIES

Desirable equipment and facilities contribute to the effective youth program of the local church. With more young people crowding into the junior high departments of our churches, you must make adequate provision for all the young people, for the church school, youth fellowship meetings, and other activities.

The trend is toward the multiple use of available space. The use of a large assembly room with its required chairs, and a set of classrooms with a second set of chairs, may become both expensive and prohibitive. One alternative is a large all-purpose room to be used for common worship of the youth department; and also for the class session, meeting around tables or in circles, in that same room, using the same chairs. Partitions or curtains may help but are not essential. For junior high classes, more isolation is recommended. The other alternative is to have a room for each class, each seating twenty to twenty-five persons. The worship, study, and other activities can take place here without going into or out of an all-youth department assembly.

For the evening youth fellowship meeting, a room is desirable which will hold the total group compactly, sitting in chairs, preferably in a circle or in a semi-circle, or in concentric rows of a circle or semi-circle. If necessary, a large room may be made smaller by closing in an area with movable partitions. In the all-purpose room, the chairs can be moved away for recreation and other space-consuming activities. The same room can be used for both church school and youth fellowship meetings. The church looking toward new structures and additions should seek professional help on this subject.

The growing youth program can be better served with adequate facilities and equipment. The minimum equipment would include such tools as the chalkboard, bulletin board, and turnover charts. The items for the worship center may be placed on a table or concealed by a curtain or behind hinged doors. There should be a library of resource material with a browsing table nearby, and an easily accessible shelf of recreational supplies. For larger pieces of recreational equipment, a closet or cabinet may be necessary. A filecase for permanent records and for charts and maps is useful.

Have ready access to audio-visual equipment, including the record player. Equip the multi-purpose room with its own kitchenette, if the room is not already near a kitchen. A fireplace and a coke machine will increase the informal and attractive atmosphere. Provide a large rugged table for meetings and other activities.

Discourage the exclusive use of any given room in a church for one or another organization, such as the scout room, or the choir room. Appropriate storage space for each organization and group should make every room in the church available for active use during the week. Above all, we must make the young people feel that the church wants them in its program, that facilities and equipment are provided, and that personnel and funds can be obtained.

CHAPTER ELEVEN

Ventures in Youth Work

RECENT EXPERIENCES in senior high youth programs indicate a decided trend toward the use of small-group units. One instance of this trend is the "cube group" approach, described and analyzed below.

THE CUBE GROUP PLAN

A local church reported that it had thirty persons who regularly attended the Sunday church school in the senior high department. The department included a large number of the ninth and tenth grade, and a few of the eleventh and twelfth grade. One teacher taught this large group, and found it difficult to maintain attention and to secure adequate discussion.

This church had an evening youth fellowship, but only fifteen or sixteen active members. The officers who planned and conducted the meetings were usually the older eleventh and twelfth graders. The ninth and tenth graders dominated the attendance, yet found the meetings unexciting to them. A careful survey indicated that a total of fifty-five persons of this age were actually related to the church membership.

The cube group plan was recommended and adopted. The name "cube" was applied to the small-group units, since the cube is a three-dimensional figure, indicating the concept of a relationship between the persons within the group and also of the presence of God in their midst. This is the plan.

(1) *The active members are divided into units of about seven or eight persons, based first upon school grade and age, then on geography or interest.* If the persons live in a wide area, those from the north side would be in one cube, those from the east side in another, and so on. If the young people attend different high schools, those from the same schools would be placed in the same cube. If there is a basketball team, an established clique, a group with very definite interests, they would be formed into a cube. Boys and girls would normally be mixed in the cubes.

(2) *To each group is assigned a counselor, a person slightly older than the members in the group.* An older youth, young adult, young married couple, or some such person who is from five to ten years older than the group would be desirable. In all activities of the cube, the counselor is involved.

(3) *To each group are assigned two inactive persons who normally would be related to the youth program.* For every function, meeting, activity, and class session of the cube, special effort is made to seek out and invite these two inactive persons. As soon as they become active, two additional inactive persons are assigned to the cube. Thus the cube is always reaching out to one or two inactive persons.

(4) *The division into cube membership can best be made by a small committee of adult leaders, church school teachers, and youth leaders.* Full consideration should be given to personality traits, interests, and other peculiarities of the young people which would tend to knit the members into a workable group. One should not hesitate to separate girl-girl and boy-girl combinations, as long as the base of division is maintained.

(5) *The memberships in the several cubes are reviewed and reshuffled twice each year,* to take into account the loss and gain in membership. Always, the best workable unit is from six to ten young persons and one counselor.

(6) *The counselors are responsible to a youth director who coordinates the activities of the whole youth program in the church.* The counselor is committed for the six-month period during which a cube is maintained, and he may be excused or re-assigned depending upon his availability and interest. The youth director, or adult adviser, has a long-term responsibility to provide continuity.

(7) *Each cube is a Sunday morning church school class.* A member of the cube prepares the lesson of the day, and conducts the discussion. The counselor will also be prepared, but his role is that of resource person, not that of teacher. Each Sunday a new cube member presents and conducts the class period. Opportunities for free inquiry and search are encouraged. Additional resource persons may be brought in upon invitation of the young person whose turn it is to lead.

(8) *The cube meets in one of the homes of its members on Sunday evening.* Thus there are as many simultaneous meetings as there are cubes. These cube meetings in private homes are held on alternate meeting nights, and different homes are used for every meeting. Such a cube meeting has the elements of worship, study, and recreation, just as any other youth fellowship meeting.

(9) *On the other alternate meeting nights, the total youth fellowship group of all the cubes meets at the church.* The program for that evening is conducted by one of the cubes.

This is the basic pattern for the operation of the cube group plan. But let us explore the other possibilities.

(10) *Each cube is encouraged to choose one of the five commissions or program areas for its own specialty.* They may find that several meetings are required to survey the possibilities before they can agree on their choice. Several cubes may choose the same commission or program area. Within each commis-

sion and program area are several items which can be seriously pursued and studied.

(11) *Each cube is urged to specialize in some activity,* such as recreational leadership, fellowship singing, drama, choral speech, puppetry, parlor games, folk games, crafts, mission study, Bible study, service project, and any other. One or two of the cube members may have a flair for one of these, and will introduce the activity to the rest. The cube might make itself proficient in the field, and then share this interest with the total youth fellowship group.

(12) *Each cube must prepare a youth fellowship meeting program.* On a schedule agreed upon, and perhaps on a topic assigned to them, or on one which the members choose out of their specialized interest, they will plan and present a complete youth fellowship program of worship, topic, and recreation.

(13) *Each cube is encouraged to go on outings, picnics, swims, excursions, skating parties, and other suitable and appropriate functions of their own choosing.* Of course, in each instance, the counselor goes along. Such activities must be cleared with the youth director to see that they do not conflict with the over-all program.

(14) *Each cube ought to undertake one major service project on its own during the half-year of its existence.* This should be apart from any major service project which the whole youth fellowship may do.

(15) *The cube meeting in different private homes exposes the young people to the parents of those homes.* Their hospitality and refreshments are graciously received. The period of socializing should not include watching television, listening to records, or dancing in the rumpus room downstairs. The cube meeting itself should be quite orderly, punctual, and disciplined. One hour might be adequate for a cube meeting in a home. At

a cube meeting, plans and assignments can be worked out. Every effort should be made to discuss subjects and topics of concern to cube members, who take turns in presenting the topic discussion of the evening. All the resources recommended for youth fellowship meetings should be available for this purpose.

(16) *It is possible that some issue or project which one cube has explored, needs support and participation by all young people of the total youth fellowship.* Some survey or inquiry, a work project or youth evangelism program, or other possibilities may be introduced.

(17) *There are no officers within the cube group except for a rotating chairman in charge of the cube meeting.* The total youth fellowship maintains its usual organization, with officers and relationships to the congregation and denomination. There is no transaction of funds within the cubes. Any expenditure would be for the total group.

While these items suggest the essence and structure of the cube group plan, the following factors make it especially attractive for adaptation in our churches.

EVALUATION OF THE PLAN

Under the cube group plan, every person immediately belongs, and is expected to share in all the cube activities. He has a share in its decisions, planning and execution of the class session, cube meeting, and other functions. He is accepted for what he is, with all his peculiar strength and weakness.

The cube group plan protects the older teenagers from being overwhelmed by the younger teenagers. To keep the eleventh and twelfth grade persons in a cube for their age means to maintain a normal social level and to assure intellectual capacity for pertinent and interesting discussion.

When a large group of junior highs enter the youth fellowship, they will have a program more adapted to their understanding if they are kept in small cube groups of their age mates.

In a large church which has fifty or more senior highs, the cube group is sure to hold attendance and interest. There will be no fringe or occasional members. Either every person is actively related in a cube, or is an inactive person who is being pursued continually by the cube to which he belongs.

When a friend or a newcomer drops in, he can be included temporarily in a cube appropriate to him and later be assigned permanently. There is always the effort to reach out to the unchurched, the inactive, the fringe group.

In the more intimate cube group, the problems and concerns which face the individual members can be more honestly shared and discussed. After a period of time, they will know each other so well that they can give strength to each other.

The particular strength of the cube system lies in the experience that a definite group of persons has in a continuous program of study, worship, work, and play, in different settings and situations, over a long period of time. This is the redemptive society: a group whose members become concerned for each other's welfare, and which is affected and changed by this love and feeling of each for the other.

While we might assume that most teenagers enjoy a normal boy-girl social life, for those who fail to achieve friendship and dates the cube provides ample opportunity to share in co-ed experiences.

There is the danger that we are making several social clubs which can become cliques. The necessity for constant inquiry and activity, for sharing and reaching out, for facing personal dilemmas and problems in an atmosphere of Christian concern, makes it more likely that the group will arrive at new and higher motives in life.

The key to the cube group is the counselor. This kind of person may seem elusive and hard to find. The counselor may not understand his role in the cube. He may not know enough of the youth program, of group discipline, of conducting discussions. The church may look to its older youth and young adult members as prospective counselors.

Though no mention has been made of the Sunday morning worship service, it is assumed that regular attendance at church service is fundamental to good Christian living.

Parents of teenagers come into the picture quite naturally, as cube meetings are held in the homes of its members.

There is really no conflict with the commission or program area plan. The cube system provides the vehicle through which the substance and content of the program areas are conveyed.

This then is the breadth and depth of the total strategy of using the small-group technique, involving every active and potential young person in the life of the church.

THE YOUTH GUIDANCE COMMITTEE

During the high school years, the average young person passes through one major crisis after another in deciding which way his life should be directed. Questions such as these are sure to arise by the time each teenager is graduated from high school:

• What kind of work am I fit to do?
• What kind of preparation and education do I need for the kind of work I want to do?
• Shoud I get married before I graduate from high school?
• Can I plan for both career and marriage?
• What is the advantage of attending a church-related college?
• Where do I find information on studying for the ministry, or to enter the mission field?
• Is there scholarship money available?
• What will military service mean to me?

- Ought I to be a conscientious objector?
- What is it like to leave home and friends and familiar places?

These are some of the countless questions young people are apt to ask. Boiled down, they involve jobs, marriage, college, military service, and family life. To meet these questions satisfactorily within the congregational family, and to give young people the benefit of a Christian interpretation and attitude in facing these problems, would your local church establish a Youth Guidance Committee?

This committee might be composed of five or more adult persons, each of whom will assume a special responsibility within the committee. We envision a long term of five to ten years' membership, perhaps with replacements being made every two years. Presumably, these committee members should be active members of the congregation, but not already carrying too many responsibilities. The special assignments may include the following:

(1) *One member specializes in the realm of vocational counseling.* This does not mean that he is a vocational counselor, but that he makes himself a veritable library of available sources of information. He should know whether the local school system provides any testing services, what happens in the interpretation of these tests, and how much personal counseling each pupil gets. He should be alert to other agencies in the community where professional vocational counseling is available. If the church and the denomination have some service in this field, he should know the facts.

(2) *Another member becomes an "expert" on colleges, universities, trade schools, nursing schools, business and other specialized institutions.* He will be especially interested in his denominational church-related colleges, and will accumulate catalogs on most of these schools. Such a person is called the "student work secretary" in some churches.

(3) *One member should know the work opportunities in his community,* depending upon the industries and economy of the locality. A person with wide contacts, with knowledge of business and persons, should prove helpful in evaluating inquiries concerning summer work opportunities, or jobs to secure upon high school graduation.

(4) *One person may become a general marriage counselor.* Such a person should be approachable, tactful, and convincing in discussing the many implications and involvements of marriage and family life, of money and in-law complications, of housing and child-caring duties. When young people become involved in unmarried pregnancy, this counselor will be available for immediate guidance. He may also concern himself with the social adjustment of teenage young people who do not appear to make the proper contacts readily.

(5) *Some person with experience in military service can be helpful in discussing the many possibilities facing a young person considering military service.* The alternatives before the teenager, including that of being a conscientious objector, and the several consequences of his choice might be reviewed.

(6) *It is entirely reasonable for one member to accept concern for the securing of scholarship funds,* either from established channels, or from individual sources within the congregational membership.

(7) *Another function may be to keep in periodic contact with those who are temporarily away from the home scene,* in military service, college, work, or for other reasons.

These committee members are not presumed to be experts or authorities in their chosen field, but merely a group of persons whose love and concern for young people and their decisions are so vital that they are willing to specialize in these areas. Frequently one or another may be professionally trained, but their participation in this committee is wholly voluntary and non-professional.

It may appear at first glance that this is quite an intrusion into the private lives of young people. One might properly argue that the normal procedure is for teenagers to find their own destiny, and to take the consequences of their decisions. The church, however, is interested in the stewardship of life, and rightfully tries to apply the best information available in motivating and directing young lives toward the most creative and satisfying decisions.

Let us follow the workings of such a committee. Together with their parents, all young persons in the tenth year of schooling, either individually or in groups of four or five, meet with this committee. Some general discussion of future plans is held, and an information card on each person is filled out. The members of the commitee point out the areas in which each can give help, and assure the young people that they are available for personal conference and consultation at any time.

The committee meets with each person again in his junior year in high school, when more specific ideas and hopes are expressed. The young person may follow this meeting by personal conference with any one of the committee members.

Finally, in his senior year, or sooner if his plans are clearly established, he may meet with the individual committee members from time to time, until all plans are set. While the initiative is taken by the committee in the young person's first visit with this group, subsequent contacts are made at the option of the young person. It is necessary, of course, that all conferences be confidential, that the best rules of personal counseling prevail, and that ultimately the young person himself make his own decision at every point.

In a delicate yet significant ministry of this kind, the relationship among the adults who serve on this committee must be of utter devotion and Christian compassion. The hopes and dreams of parents, the insights and knowledge of teachers and advisers, the prayers and the love of the minister must be coordinated into a unified approach for each teenager. This offer and availability of service must be flexible and attractive, with nothing to indicate coercion or pressure. With time and experience, both committee members and young people may find within the range of this committee's activities the elements of true Christian community.

When the high school graduate is congratulated in the name of the church, the minister knows that the full strength of the congregation was behind the plans made by the graduate for his immediate future. The church which renders this service will hold its young people through and beyond high school graduation. The concept of Christian vocation which dominated all these deliberations should find fulfillment in the mature Christian person thus released into the world.

THE RANGE OF EXPERIENCE

People differ in their readiness to undertake new experiences. A teenager, for instance, cannot observe personal devotions without knowing something about worship and prayer. Learning about worship and prayer involves basic instruction. It calls for participation in church life where he observes and experiences both the spirit and the content of worship and prayer.

Recognizing that growth and maturity require step-by-step development, your church can chart its youth program on a phase-by-phase progression. This assumes that your church maintains an aggressive and consistent program including church school classes, youth fellowship meetings, and other appropriate activities. Your responsible adult leaders must have some clear ideas about the goals and objectives of your church's youth program. What do you expect to happen to your teenager in four to six years?

If it is agreed that one important objective of the youth

program is to prepare the young adolescent for mature Christian adulthood, then your year-to-year program has a long-term perspective. There must be deliberate and increasing demands with more challenging experiences for the growing teenager. The progression can integrate the suggestions outlined in this book. Your program then recognizes age-group expectations, and provides evaluation of progress for the individual as well as for the group.

The following descriptions of experiences are suggestive, and indicate those things which happen around and to the person. This is not an attempt to measure "spiritual growth" or the "degree of commitment" or even his "knowledge of the Bible." Obviously, the hope is that every teenager in your church may progress through the three phases: *the beginner, the regular, the mature Christian.* With each additional venture, his range of experiences becomes both wider and more profound. Progress may be achieved earlier in some areas than in others. The five program areas of the commission plan are used as a basis for the descriptions.

PHASE ONE — THE BEGINNER

In this phase, the young person embarks on a series of experiences leading toward Christian maturity and adult churchmanship. In the true sense of the word, he is a beginner. Perhaps in age, he is a junior high person, but he may be older. We can assume, therefore, that the most elementary experiences are reasonable for him.

He should be able to attend with satisfaction a meeting or class or the church service. Under coaxing, his attendance may be fairly regular. Essentially he comes as a passive spectator, hoping that he will not be imposed upon. For this reason, an interesting or entertaining speaker, a fascinating film, a general program, a "good discussion," appeal to him most.

He is present for social occasions of food and play, both

indoor and outdoor. But he is not prepared, and for that matter not willing, to take even a little share of responsibility, whether for reading Scripture or for cleaning up. When he is pressed, he may read a chapter or a book which others may also be reading. During hymn singing at church or fellowship singing in the youth group, his participation is minimum.

He hates most when his knowledge of the Bible or of Christian faith is tested. Words like stewardship and commitment, grace and salvation, are beyond him. He has no idea about his denomination, its history or its missionary enterprise. His financial gifts are in the nickel and dime stage. When he smells work, he is busy elsewhere. On this basis, the following are the experiences that may be expected of him in the program areas.

Christian Faith

The beginner reads a book or two on Christian beliefs. He studies the essentials of church membership and may be received into communicant membership. The wide implications of the Christian gospel amaze him a bit, and he is appalled at the demands of commitment and stewardship. Nevertheless he attends church activities as faithfully as he can, though school, friends, and home are always pressing for his time. By and large, his contribution to any discussion on personal conduct is superficial and ordinary. He becomes slightly aware of the denomination of his church, yet speaks of the Roman Catholic church as "another denomination." He needs to learn the fundamentals of Christian worship and prayer.

Christian Witness

The beginner saw a film on stewardship. It was entertaining, but he didn't give the subject a second thought. The word evangelism was repulsive, so he dismissed that, too. But probably the fact that he sings in the youth choir can be credited to churchmanship. He does sing a nice tenor, and there are social times after choir practice, too. The church school lesson on

Christian vocations didn't register at all. He wasn't sure what he wanted to be, and anyway, he wasn't thinking of being a minister.

Christian Outreach

When his church held a mission study institute, the beginner was faintly aware of something "home" and "foreign," but he couldn't tell the difference. There was a large display of pictures and books, trinkets and objects. There was even a song sung in a foreign language, and a filmstrip story about some child in a foreign land. He did enjoy "trick or treat" at Hallowe'en because his youth group collected money for UNICEF, and old clothes for overseas relief. His church school lesson on United Nations was helpful, because he was studying about U.N. at school that same week.

Christian Citizenship

There was a work project at church, the beginner learned, but he didn't want to get himself splattered with paint. He did let himself get into taking odd jobs on Christ's Workday. It was awkward to have all this talk about race relations in the church school lessons, but he went along with it. But that part about the strike at the plant burned him up. He had heard his father lecture on the subject at dinner the other night. Imagine the youth discussing Christianity and politics—they were two topics quite removed from each other. He sat through the stupid meeting.

Christian Fellowship

To the beginner, this program area meant recreation and boy-girl. On both subjects he was eager and willing. He didn't miss a party, nor any of the refreshments. He absorbed all the discussion on dating do's and don'ts, and permitted himself to buy a copy of "Dating Data." He couldn't quite make out why sex was even mentioned at church, though he did realize that boy-girl eventually lead to family life. He wasn't happy about it, but the beginner got roped in on the Christmas pageant, where he was well hidden by the costume and make-up.

Phase Two — The Regular

By the time the person has entered Phase Two, he is more active in the life of the church. His attendance and participation is indeed regular. His gifts and work reflect deeper appreciation of his church membership.

Probably the most observable feature of this phase is his participation beyond the local church, in summer camps and conferences, in youth rallies, in denominational activities. Senior high persons who have had the advantages of the range of experiences in Phase One are now ready for Phase Two activities.

Again, quick acknowledgment is made that inner convictions and spiritual grasp are not under judgment. The youth program can only provide setting, invoke divine guidance, and challenge young people to wholesome growth. Here then are the program areas and the range of experiences in Phase Two.

Christian Faith

The regular is fairly comfortable in a discussion on faith and belief, on prayer and the Bible. He is able to prepare and conduct a meaningful worship service. He is acutely aware of his denominational heritage, and in fact, has done some personal research for a school assignment. The many moral dilemmas at school bother him, especially cheating, vandalism, drinking, and the talk of free sex-play. He heard a sermon on commitment that brought new awareness of its implications in his personal life. His was a big moment when on Youth Sunday, he read a prayer at the morning service. Since last summer, he has been observing personal devotions at home, and insists on table grace at the family dinner table.

Christian Witness

At the youth rally, the regular was quite impressed by the talk about fellowship-evangelism, of young people calling on others. This was beyond him, but it was reassuring to hear these teenagers tell of their exciting experiences. This year, he didn't throw away his box of offering envelopes. In fact, he did make a pledge, his first time. At summer camp he heard about the work of his denomination and of his responsibility to it. Taking communion at church has become a thrilling experience. When he was discussion leader on Christian vocation, he learned for the first time that a person can choose to make any honest work his Christian calling.

Christian Outreach

The regular was responsible for book-reviewing a mission study book, and was surprised to learn that his denomination was doing home mission work in his own state. At summer camp was a youth leader who attended a world conference of Christian youth. This seemed remote but he was willing to accept the fact that somehow his own home church was related to something around the world. The United Nations Day observance at church was presented by the young people, and the regulars conducted the whole affair.

Christian Citizenship

The regular has learned that church activities can include physical work. What surprised him was that working together brought people closer together. So he welcomed the opportunity to do door-to-door survey in the new housing development. The churches in town wanted to know what religious preferences the people had. The youth group conducted a series of discussions about other groups of people in their town: Negroes, Catholics, Jews, war-brides, and others. This called for visits and speakers, and for awhile the attendance maintained a new high. The rash of juvenile delinquency stories in the paper was cause for a special study, and the youth group visited a juvenile court to get facts for intelligent discussion.

Christian Fellowship

One major change since the regular came back from summer conference is the way young people now take a more friendly attitude to the home church. Why, the young people found courage to ask the church council to permit folk dancing at youth meetings. The big event of the month was to entertain the annual youth rally of the region. That so many people belong to his own denomination impressed him anew. The hobby show last spring started several persons on new interests. The most popular books in the youth fellowship library appear to be the ones on boy-girl relations. That lively meeting on mixed marriage seemed to answer a lot of questions. And now the parents take turns serving refreshments. Perhaps that father-son banquet paved the way for this.

PHASE THREE — THE MATURE CHRISTIAN

There is probably no person who "arrives" in Christian maturity. The maturing process goes on and on, and the alert churchman is the first to admit his need of continued spiritual growth. Thus the young people in the late teen-years who have experienced Phase Two activities can now cope with those of Phase Three.

Not only is the mature Christian a stalwart regular, he is willing to plunge into daring ventures in full confidence that God expects great things of him. He sees the mission of the church as something beyond human powers, yet with human responsibilties. The work of interdenominational and ecumenical movements becomes significant and relevant.

The concept of Christian vocation makes him restless and eager. He gives far more of his time and money to the work of the church, often to the consternation of his contemporaries. The disciplines of the Christian life, such as tithing, devotions, and compassion become an integral part of his life. Thus he is willing and able to consider these Phase Three experiences.

Christian Faith

The mature Christian is alive to the implications of the Christian gospel and keeps raising new and profound questions on such issues as "What is man?" and "How can I respond to the love of God?" He is becoming a junior theologian, especially since he can expound at the prayer cell meetings every Tuesday night at 9. At the recent spiritual life retreat, he was very helpful in defining his position on gambling and gossiping. Having attended the recent United Christian Youth conference, he is proud of his denomination, yet fully conscious that his is one of many, working together for the kingdom of God.

Christian Witness

Twice this past year, the mature Christian called on un-churched young people. The first time was with the whole youth group when the churches of the town carried out a combined youth-evangelism program. The other day he went out again with two others, to make what he called "follow-up visits." His insistence on increased giving of money is matched by the long hours he gives helping at the vacation church school. A new privilege is his, since he became youth member on the church's committee on Christian education. When he finally selected his life work, he had talked with the minister about the Christian commitment in his future line of work.

Christian Outreach

The mature Christian arranged for his church school class to visit the home missions center in his state. This first-hand visit was very revealing, and now the study books became full of meaning. Even the money-gifts increased. This year, he is saving money to apply for overseas ecumenical work-camp under the World Council of Churches. He has not yet recovered from talking with the overseas missionary at last summer's youth conference. The paper he wrote for school on world order and peace was a superb job, since he wrote it after a visit to the United Nations building in New York City. Twice his youth group went to the clothing center of Church World Service to sort and pack relief clothing for overseas shipment.

Christian Citizenship

The youth group at his church held a joint planning weekend retreat with the young people of the Negro church in town. There were many misgivings among the parents, but the young people had a good time. The mature Christian was selected as a delegate to the U.C.Y.M. citizenship seminar at the state capitol, and since then has become a loud supporter of Christians-in-politics. He has a standing offer with the minister to give transportation for any church member or dignitary, provided, of course, that his jalopy is an acceptable vehicle.

Christian Fellowship

The atmosphere at church has a new tone since the three-part Parent-Youth Series was held. People are more friendly, especially the older folks to the teenagers. And since the minister completed the six-weeks Thursday discussions on Preparation for Marriage, the going-steady pressure has been eased. The young people seem more relaxed. The recreation program is better, too, both at the church's teen-town and at the Sunday night meetings. Sending the mature Christian to the recreational laboratory has helped. He hasn't been the same since he went to the United Christian Youth Movement's training conference last summer. He served on the community U.C.Y.M. council which sponsored Youth Week activities. The latest in the creative arts department is rhythmic choir — even the boys are doing it. And thanks to the mature Christian, the young people remember the boys and girls in college, in uniform, and away, with birthday cards, letters, and gifts.

Bibliography

About Myself by Nevin C. Harner. Christian Education Press, 1950.
A common sense guide to self-understanding, against a background of psychology and religion.

The Adolescent in Your Family, Children's Bureau Publication 347, Washington, D. C., Revised 1955.
Pamphlet giving some of the underlying needs of young people.

The American Teenager, by Remmers and Radler, Bobbs Merrill Co., 1957.
Statistics and unsigned letters reveal teenage concerns, attitudes and actions.

Careers for You by Erma Paul Ferrari. Abingdon-Cokesbury, 1953.
Sound, specific vocational guidance in the light of Christian faith.

The Church School, by Paul H. Vieth, Christian Education Press, 1957.
Helpful discussion on such areas as awards, church and home, curriculum, discipline, teaching, and worship.

Facts of Life and Love for Teenagers by Evelyn M. Duvall. Association Press, Revised 1956.
To help young people face squarely the facts of life.

Guiding Youth in Christian Growth by Oliver deWolf Cummings. The Judson Press, 1954.
To help leaders of youth see that intelligent effort and Christian commitment can accomplish much for young people. Prepared as a leadership training text.

Handbook for Recreation, Children's Bureau Publication 231, Washington, 1960.
Comprehensive and helpful book for recreation of all sorts, mixers, circle and line games, active and quiet games, etc.

How a Small Church Can Have Good Christian Education by Virgil E. Foster. Harper & Bros., 1956.
Practical examples, direct help on the total Christian educational program, as well as specifics in the youth field.

How to Help People by Rudolph M. Wittenberg. Association Press, 1953.

A handbook on practical questions of lay workers who counsel young people. This is a popular condensation of *So You Want to Help People*.

How to Live With Your Teen-Ager by Dorothy W. Baruch, McGraw-Hill, 1953.

Especially for parents, but helpful for all workers with youth in presenting a basic understanding of teenagers and guideposts for living with them.

I Believe by Nevin C. Harner. Christian Education Press, 1950.

Friendly, informal discussion of major questions concerning the Christian faith of young people.

If You Marry Outside Your Faith by James A. Pike. Harper & Bros., 1954.

Clears misconceptions and provides a solution about mixed marriages, stating religious positions and implications.

In One Spirit by D. Campbell Wyckoff. Friendship Press, 1957.

The philosophy and ways of handling senior highs and missions.

It's Worth Your Life by Erma Paul Ferrari. Friendship Press, 1955.

Vocational pamphlet describing opportunities for youth in the Christian world mission.

Leadership of Teen-Age Groups by Dorothy M. Roberts. Association Press, 1950.

Ways in which understanding adults can counsel teen-agers as individuals and groups.

Learning Together in the Christian Fellowship by Sara Little, John Knox Press, 1956.

Practical and stimulating book on group study and group dynamics.

Living with Parents, by Grace Sloan Overton. Broadman Press, 1954.

Problems of growing up—dating, vocations, home-making, religion, all discussed by a well known youth counselor.

The Objective of Christian Education for Senior High Young People, Division of Christian Education, National Council of Churches, 1958.
   Helpful background discussion and description of Christian youth in relation to the Christian education objective.

A Study of Adolescents, Boy Scouts of America, New Brunswick, N. J., 1955.
   A study of boys, especially interesting to those concerned with the problems of middle adolescence.

The Teacher and Young Teens by Louise B. Griffths, Bethany Press, 1954.
   Basic understanding of junior highs and work of church. Excellent chapters on tools for teaching.

Teen-Agers by Gladys Gardner Jenkins, W. W. Bauer, Helen S. Shacter. Scott, Foresman & Company, 1954.
   Helps 14-, 15-, 16-year olds in particular learn ways of working toward good health—physical, mental, and social.

Teen-Agers—Their Days and Ways by Rowena Ferguson. National Council of Churches of Christ, 1952.
   Pamphlet to help adult leaders in the church understand young people.

Use of Audio Visuals in the Church by Oscar J. Rumpf, Christian Education Press, 1958.
   How to use audio-visuals effectively in the church for each age-group.

Ways Youth Learn by Clarice M. Bowman. Harper & Bros., 1952.
   A practical guide for adult leaders on the best methods for presenting the Christian faith to young people.

Whose World? A Handbook on International Relations by John Wood, Friendship Press, 1960.
   Describes revolutionary forces in today's world; defines young Christian's responsibility and role in international relations.

Wide As the World, Junior High and Missions by Louise B. Griffths. Friendship Press, 1957.
   Philosophy and methods in missionary education of junior highs.

Your Faith and Your Life Work by Elmer G. Million, Friendship Press, 1960.
   Presents "Christian vocation," God calling every Christian to a life of witness and service.

The Youth Fellowship by Oliver deWolf Cummings. The Judson Press, 1956.

A leadership training text for those who work with youth to give understanding and tested plans of the Youth Fellowship.

Youth Looks at the Church by Helen F. Spaulding. National Council of Churches of Christ, 1956.

Pamphlet reporting results of a study of the effectiveness of youth work in churches.

Youth, the Years from Ten to Sixteen by Arnold Gesell, Frances L. Ilg, Louise B. Ames. Harper & Bros., 1956.

Studies of a selected group of normal, middle class adolescents, showing year by year changes as growth happens.

Regular publications by Friendship Press, 257 Fourth Ave., New York 10, N. Y.

Each year books and guides, plays, and visuals for use with junior highs and senior highs are prepared for the two mission study themes.

Pamphlet Series

Public Affairs pamphlets like *Too Young to Marry, Keeping Up with Teenagers, Coming of Age: Problems of Teen-agers* are being published regularly, are inexpensive, and deal with current interests.

ADDRESS: 22 East 38th Street, New York 16, N. Y.

Science Research Associates produces three types of pamphlets:

(1) Junior Life Adjustment Booklets for pre-teen and early teen young people. Sample titles: *How to Get Along with Others, Planning Your Job Future, Learning About Sex.*

(2) Life Adjustment Booklets for teenage readers. Sample titles: *Dating Days, Understanding the Other Sex, Your Personality and Your Job.*

(3) Better Living Booklets for teachers, counselors, and parents. Sample titles: *Let's Listen to Youth, Helping Brothers and Sisters Get Along, Helping Youth Choose Careers.*

ADDRESS: 57 West Grand Avenue, Chicago 10, Illinois.

The National Education Association has been cooperating with various other agencies to prepare materials. Sample titles: *It's High Time*—Guide for Parents of High School Students, *Finding Yourself, Learning About Love.*

ADDRESS: 1201 Sixteenth Street, N.W., Washington 6, D. C.

Suggested Audio-Visuals

There is a growing list of helpful 16 mm. films (F), filmstrips (FS), and sound filmstrips (SFS) which can enrich your work with young people. The following titles suggest current material available. Secure the latest catalog for description, length, and rental prices on these and other titles from the denominational audio-visual library or Religious Film Library convenient to you.

For Use by Adult Persons, Parents, and Workers With Youth

Films

Age of Turmoil
Feeling of Hostility
Feeling of Rejection
Meaning of Adolescence
Meeting the Needs of the Adolescent
Roots of Happiness
Teaching in the Church School

Sound Filmstrips

A Friend to Youth (Youth Workers' Audio-Visual Kit)
Counseling for Church Vocations
Decision Saturday (Youth Workers' Audio-Visual Kit)
You for Youth (Youth Workers' Audio-Visual Kit)
Double Identity (Youth Workers' Audio-Visual Kit)
That Youth May Know (Youth Workers' Audio-Visual Kit)
Through Faith and Fellowship (Youth Workers' Audio-Visual Kit)
Do You Know Your Adolescents?
Teaching the Bible to High School Youth
Scouting Program in Protestant Churches
Together We Grow (Church School Administration Kit)
A Mirror to Myself (Church School Administration Kit)
How Persons Learn (Leadership Education A-V Series)
The Great Adventure (Leadership Education A-V Series)
The Growing Teacher (Leadership Education A-V Series)
The Teacher Prepares (Leadership Education A-V Series)
Built Upon a Rock (Family Life A-V Series)
For the Record (Family Life A-V Series)

194 VENTURES IN YOUTH WORK

A Harvest from Holidays (Family Life A-V Series)
No Easy Answer (Family Life A-V Series)
A Family Affair
Democracy Is Home Made
Family on Trial
Is Your Home Fun?

Filmstrips
Camping with Junior Highs
I Work with Junior Highs

FOR USE WITH YOUNG PEOPLE

Films
Appreciating Our Parents
Are You Ready for Marriage?
You and Your Family
You and Your Friends
Dating Do's and Don'ts
The Griper
The High Room
Job for Bob
What Happened to Jo-Jo?
A Date with Your Family
Make Way for Youth
The Difference
Crossroads
This Charming Couple (Marriage for Moderns Series)
Marriage Today (Marriage for Moderns Series)
Choosing for Happiness (Marriage for Moderns Series)
It Takes All Kinds (Marriage for Moderns Series)
Who's Boss? (Marriage for Moderns Series)
Shy Guy
Friendship Begins at Home
Who Is Sylvia?
Joe and Roxy

Sound Filmstrips
And With This Ring
Junior High Friendships (Preparation for Marriage Series)
How About a Date? (Preparation for Marriage Series)
Is This One for Me? (Preparation for Marriage Series)
The Meaning of Engagement (Preparation for Marriage Series)

We Have This Fellowship (Youth A-V Series)
The Faith of a Guy (Youth A-V Series)
Gallery of Witnesses (Youth A-V Series)
I Found a New World (Youth A-V Series)
The Measure of a Man (Youth A-V Series)
How Wide Is Our Circle? (Youth A-V Series)
Big Enough to Tackle (Youth A-V Series)
The Accused
A Job for Jimmy Cooper
Do You Dig Friendship?

Religious Film Libraries

The Religious Film Libraries is an interdenominational organization which sponsors a network of film rental libraries. Headquarters are as follows:

17 Park Place, New York 7, New York

1501 Race Street, Philadelphia 2, Pennsylvania

Room 505, Arrott Building, Fourth and Wood Streets, Pittsburgh 22, Pennsylvania

8 North Sixth Street, Richmond 9, Virginia

57 East Main Street, Columbus 15, Ohio

240 Fifth Street, Dayton 2, Ohio

220 South Downey Avenue, Indianapolis 7, Indiana

220 West Monroe Street, Chicago 6, Illinois

2445 Park Avenue, Minneapolis 4, Minnesota

Beaumont and Pine Boulevard, St. Louis 3, Missouri

4006 Live Oak Street, Dallas 4, Texas

1457 South Broadway, Denver 23, Colorado

1205 North 45th, Seattle 3, Washington

825 S.W. Fourth Avenue, Portland 4, Oregon

2408 W. Seventh Street, Los Angeles 57, California

Other Agencies and Organizations

Agencies and organizations interested in Protestant youth work have national headquarters as follows:

Anti-Defamation League of B'nai B'rith, 515 Madison Ave., New York 22, New York

Boy Scouts of America, New Brunswick, New Jersey

Broadcasting and Film Commission, 220 Fifth Ave., New York 1, New York

Camp Fire Girls, Inc., 16 E. 48th St., New York 17, N. Y.

Church World Service, 475 Riverside Drive, New York 27, N. Y.

Friendship Press (Joint Commission on Missionary Education), 257 Fourth Ave., New York 10, New York

Girl Scouts of the U.S.A., 155 E. 44th St., New York 17, New York

International Christian Youth Exchange, 475 Riverside Drive, New York 27, N. Y.

National Council of Churches of Christ in the U.S.A., 297 Fourth Ave., New York 10, New York

UNESCO Publication Service, 475 Fifth Ave., New York 17, New York

United Christian Youth Movement, 257 Fourth Ave., New York 10, New York

United Fellowship of Protestants, 122 Maryland Ave., N.W., Washington 2, D. C.

United Student Christian Council, 257 Fourth Ave., New York 10, New York

Visual Education Fellowship, 257 Fourth Ave., New York 10, New York

World Council of Churches, Youth Department, 156 Fifth Ave., New York 10, New York

World Council of Christian Education and Sunday School Association, 156 Fifth Ave., New York 10, N. Y.

Young Men's Christian Association, 291 Broadway, New York 7, New York

Young Women's Christian Association, 600 Lexington Ave., New York 22, New York

Denominational Headquarters

The following is a list of addresses of denominations cooperating in the United Christian Youth Movement. In each case, address inquiries to the director of youth work.

African Methodist Episcopal Church, 414 Eighth Avenue, South, Nashville 3, Tennessee

African Methodist Episcopal Zion Church, 126 Atlantic Street, Hackensack, New Jersey

American Baptist Convention, 1703 Chestnut Street, Philadelphia 3, Pennsylvania

American Evangelical Lutheran Church, Grand View College, Des Moines 16, Iowa

Associate Reformed Presbyterian Church, 113 West Eleventh Street, Charlotte 6, North Carolina

Augustana Evangelical Lutheran Church, 2445 Park Avenue, Minneapolis 4, Minnesota

Church of the Brethren, 1451 Dundee Street, Elgin, Illinois

Church of Christ, Holiness, U. S. A., 44th Street and St. Lawrence, Chicago, Illinois

Church of God, Box 67, 1303 E. Fifth Street, Anderson, Indiana

Churches of God in North America, 13th and Walnut Streets, Harrisburg, Pennsylvania

Christian Methodist Episcopal Church, 4043 Drexel Blvd., Chicago, Illinois

Cumberland Presbyterian Church, Box 5535, 1987 Union Avenue, Memphis 4, Tennessee

Disciples of Christ, International Convention, 222 South Downey Avenue, Indianapolis 7, Indiana

Evangelical United Brethren Church, 601 West Riverview, Dayton 6, Ohio

Five Year Meeting of Friends, 101 Quaker Hill Drive, Richmond, Indiana

The Methodist Church, Box 871, Nashville 2, Tennessee

Moravian Church in America, 79 West Church Street, Bethlehem, Pennsylvania

National Baptist Convention, Inc., 330 Charlotte Avenue, Nashville 3, Tennessee

Presbyterian Church in the United States, 8 North Sixth Street, Richmond 9, Virginia

Protestant Episcopal Church, 28 Havemeyer Place, Greenwich, Connecticut

Reformed Church in 'America, Room 1804, 475 Riverside Drive, New York 27, New York

Seventh Day Baptist Church, Alfred Station, New York

United Church of Christ: (Evangelical and Reformed Church) 1505 Race Street, Philadelphia 2, Pennsylvania; (Congregational Christian Churches) 14 Beacon Street, Boston 8, Massachusetts

United Presbyterian Church in the United States of America, Witherspoon Building, Philadelphia 7, Pennsylvania

United Lutheran Church in 'America (Luther League of America), 2900 Queen Lane, Philadelphia 29, Pennsylvania